100
CLEVER CRAFTS

100
Clever Crafts

Sebastian Kelly

HOW TO USE THE MEASUREMENTS

All craftspeople have their own way of working and feel most comfortable calculating in their preferred measurements. So, where applicable, the option of metric, imperial and cup measures are given. The golden rule is to choose only one set of measurements and to stick with it throughout each project to ensure accurate results.

PUBLISHER'S NOTE

Crafts and hobbies are great fun to learn and can fill many hours of rewarding leisure time, but some general points should be remembered for safety and care of the environment.

☞ *Always choose non-toxic materials wherever possible, for example paints, glue and varnishes. Where these are not suitable, use materials in a well-ventilated area and always follow the manufacturer's instructions.*

☞ *Craft knives, needles, scissors sewing machines and all sharp implements should be used with care. Always use a cutting board or mat to avoid damage to household surfaces (it is also safer to cut onto a firm, hard surface).*

☞ *Protect surfaces from paint, glue and varnish splashes by laying down old newspapers, plastic sheeting or an old sheet.*

SOME USEFUL TERMS

US	UK
Clear rubbing alcohol	*White spirit*
Flat latex	*Matt emulsion paint*
Grease pencil	*Chinagraph pencil*
Heavy-weight iron-on fabric	*Heavy pelmet vilene*
Posterboard	*Card*
Styrofoam	*Polystyrene*
Upholstery fabric	*Furnishing fabric*
White glue	*PVA glue*
Zipper	*Zip*

This edition published in 1997 by
Sebastian Kelly
2 Rectory Road
Oxford OX4 1BW

© Anness Publishing Limited 1993, 1995

Produced by Anness Publishing Limited

ISBN 1 901688 25 9

Publisher: Joanna Lorenz
Project Editor: Penelope Cream
Editorial Assistant: Charles Moxham
Designer: Hall Design
Photographer: Martin Norris
Illustrator: Vana Haggerty

Printed in Singapore by Star Standard Industries Pte. Ltd.

3 5 7 9 10 8 6 4 2

CONTENTS

CROWN BOX

This regal box with its golden crowns would be perfect for holding cufflinks or earrings. Bigger boxes could, of course, be made for larger items — perhaps envelopes and writing paper, or paintbrushes.

YOU WILL NEED
Tracing paper
Pencil
Ruler
Heavy corrugated cardboard
Craft knife
Strong clear glue
Masking tape
Newspaper
Diluted PVA glue
Fine sandpaper
Small paintbrush
Assorted poster paints
Clear gloss varnish

1 Scale up the templates for the box pieces and transfer them to the heavy cardboard. Cut out each piece with a craft knife. Glue the pieces together, and tape them in place.

2 Tear the newspaper into strips about 2.5 cm (1 in) wide. Fill a bowl with diluted PVA glue. Dip each strip of paper into the glue and stick it down onto the box framework. Overlap each strip of paper slightly, to give added strength. Cover both parts of the box with four layers of papier-mâché, and leave to dry in a warm place.

3 When the box is dry, lightly smooth its surface with fine sandpaper and prime it with two coats of white paint. Draw in the crown motifs.

4 Decorate the box with poster or gouache paints. You may wish to add definition to the design with black paint.

5 Allow the box to dry over-night, and then seal it with two coats of clear gloss varnish. Leave to dry.

Box Wall long cut 2

Box Wall cut 2

WALL SCONCE

Make this bright wall container to cheer up a corner of the kitchen. Its very simple design could be easily adapted to hold a variety of things, and it could of course be decorated to suit your own colour scheme.

YOU WILL NEED
Tracing paper
Pencil
Ruler
Heavy corrugated cardboard
Craft knife
Strong clear glue
Masking tape
Newspaper
Diluted PVA glue
Fine sandpaper
Assorted poster paints
Small paintbrush
Clear gloss varnish
Metal hanger

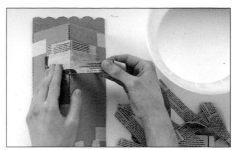

1 Scale up the templates and transfer each piece of the wall sconce to heavy corrugated cardboard. Be sure to make two side pieces! Cut out each piece of the wall sconce with a craft knife.

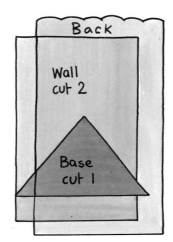

2 Glue and tape the sconce together. Tear newspaper into strips about 2.5 cm (1 in) wide. Dip each strip of paper into diluted PVA glue and then lay it onto the sconce, slightly overlapping the previous one to give added strength.

Repeat this process until you have covered the sconce. You may not be able to cover the inside completely — go down as far as you can. Apply three layers of papier-mâché. Allow to dry overnight.

3 Smooth the surface lightly with fine sandpaper, and prime it with two coats of white paint. When dry, draw on your design in pencil.

4 Start filling in the design with poster paint. You may wish to use black paint to add definition to the design.

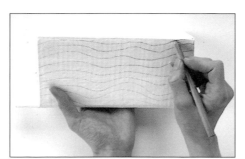

5 Allow the paint to dry thoroughly, and then seal the sconce with two coats of clear gloss varnish. When dry, stick the metal hanger to the back with strong clear glue.

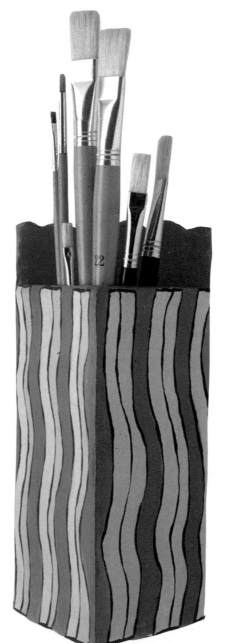

BUTTONS

If you have ever had difficulty finding just the right buttons for a hand-knitted garment, or hated the plastic ones on a jacket, then papier-mâché buttons could be the solution! Make a simple, brightly coloured set like this one, or be really adventurous and use miniature confectionery moulds to produce exotically shaped buttons.

YOU WILL NEED
Newspaper
Diluted PVA glue
Scissors
Fine sandpaper
Assorted poster paints
Small paintbrush
Darning needle
Clear gloss varnish

1 Tear the newspaper into long strips about 2.5 cm (1 in) wide. Fill a bowl with diluted PVA glue and dip a strip of paper into the glue. Allow it to soak for a few seconds, and then roughly shape it into a flat circle. Squash the circle firmly between your finger and thumb, and leave it to dry in a warm place. Make as many buttons as required.

2 Trim each dry button into a neat circle. Tear some small, thin strips of newspaper, dip into the diluted PVA glue and use to bind the edges of each button. Allow the buttons to dry.

3 Smooth the surface of each button lightly with fine sandpaper, and then apply two coats of white paint. Colour the buttons with poster paint. The mottled effect is achieved by using three uneven coats of paint, each coat being a couple of shades darker than the previous one.

4 Use a darning needle to make two or four regularly spaced holes in each button.

5 Seal the surface of each button with two coats of clear gloss varnish.

PRETTY PLATTER

This ornamental and practical platter can be used on special occasions, and is pretty enough to display in your kitchen at other times. Do remember not to wash it; just clean it by wiping it with a damp cloth.

YOU WILL NEED
Platter for a mould
Petroleum jelly
Newspaper
Wallpaper paste
Craft knife
White matt emulsion paint
Large paintbrush
Small paintbrush
Assorted poster paints
Pencil
Clear gloss varnish

1 Grease the platter with a layer of petroleum jelly. Cover the platter with at least six layers of newspaper strips soaked in wallpaper paste. Leave an overlap of 20 mm (¾ in) around the edge. Leave to dry in a warm place for at least 3 days.

2 Trim the edges with a craft knife and remove the papier-mâché shape from the platter. Do not use any force; it separates easily when it is completely dry.

Cover the edges with two layers of papier-mâché for a neat finish. Leave to dry, then prime the platter with two coats of white matt emulsion paint and leave to dry.

3 Cover the platter with a thin wash of colour and leave to dry.

4 Decorate by drawing the design onto the platter in pencil, and then very carefully paint in the design.

5 Allow the paint to dry, and then seal it with two coats of clear gloss varnish. Leave to dry overnight in a warm place.

PIGLET PUPPET

Children will love this appealing puppet which is made from inexpensive materials. Piglet's head is easy to sculpt in papier-mâché. A whole farmyard of animals can be constructed in the same way.

YOU WILL NEED
Wire coat hanger
Small plastic yogurt pot
Masking tape
Newspaper
Stiff paper
Small mixing bowl
Diluted PVA glue
Rubber-covered wire
Poster paint
Round paintbrush
Flat paintbrush
Scissors
45 cm × 30 cm (18 in × 12 in) fabric

1 Untwist a wire coat hanger and straighten it into a long length.

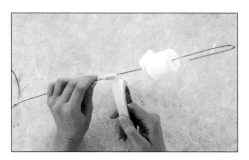

2 Make a circular base of the wire at one end. Use the remaining wire as a backbone and bend the other end into a long hook. Make a hole in the centre of the base of the yogurt pot, and slide it down over the hook until it is about 16 cm (6½ in) above the base. Secure with masking tape, and stuff it with newspaper.

3 Wrap strips of newspaper about 20 mm (¾ in) wide around the yogurt pot to form the head. Roll a small strip of stiff paper into a cylinder to form the snout and tape on.

4 Form cheeks of small balls of newspaper and attach to the head with masking tape. Dip strips of newspaper into the PVA glue and wrap them around head. Build up four layers of strips. Leave to dry overnight.

5 Cut two equal short lengths of rubber-covered wire. Bind the ends together with masking tape to form trotters. Tape onto the wire just beneath the head.

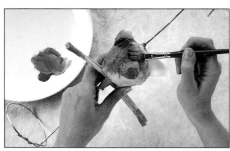

6 Cut out two ears from stiff paper and tape onto the head. Paint the head and hooves a pink pig colour, and add the details of the features. Leave to dry.

7 Cut out the robe in one piece and spread glue along the edges of the material. Make a hole for the head. Pull the robe over the pig's head, and the sleeves over the 'arms'.

EGYPTIAN MASK

Create this beautiful mask at home using professional mask makers' techniques which allow a perfect fit. You will be surprised at how easily you can produce new identities for all your friends and family.

YOU WILL NEED
Old scarf
Petroleum jelly
Paper tissues
Gummed brown paper tape
Black felt-tip pen
Diluted PVA glue
Large paintbrush
Scissors
Assorted poster paints
Small paintbrush
Fine sandpaper
Gilt wax
Soft cloth
Elastic

1 Ask the model to sit in a relaxed position. Cover the hair with an old scarf. Apply a liberal covering of petroleum jelly to the face, especially on and around the nose, eyes and eyebrows. Cover the face and eyelids with a thin layer of paper tissues.

2 Tear off strips of gummed paper tape. Make a band that passes around the forehead and fasten in place by moistening the paper. Soak small pieces of tape in water and apply them to the model's face on top of the tissues. Begin at the forehead and work down, making sure the pieces overlap slightly. Add two more layers. Smooth out any air bubbles. Cut the back of the headband and gently lift the mask away. Leave to dry overnight.

3 Coat the mask with a layer of diluted PVA glue and allow to dry. Repeat twice. Gently replace the mask on the model's head and hold in place with a vertical band of gummed paper. Draw eyeshapes around and slightly larger than the eyes with a black felt-tip pen. Take care not to go too close to the eye sockets. Gently remove the mask from the model.

4 Cut out the eye shapes. Paint the mask with white paint and sand down when dry. Paint the mask a deep red and again leave to dry.

5 Rub on a thin coat of gilt wax with a cloth, allowing the red to show through. Buff the gold using your thumb and paint a blue outline around the eyes. Make holes on the sides of the mask, thread elastic and knot.

DESIGNER BOWL

Small pieces of blue, yellow and orange paper were used to create this striking papier-mâché bowl. Try combining other colours of your choice.

YOU WILL NEED
Glass bowl
Petroleum jelly
Brightly coloured paper
Diluted PVA glue
Scissors
Large paintbrush

1 Cover the inside of a glass bowl with a layer of petroleum jelly.

2 Tear the paper into many pieces about 2.5 cm (1 in) large. Soak a few pieces of paper at a time in the diluted PVA glue. Press against the inside of the bowl, slightly overlapping each piece. Cover the whole bowl. Add a second layer, and repeat the process four or five times. Leave to dry in a warm place.

3 When the papier-mâché is thoroughly dry, remove from the bowl.

4 Touch up if necessary with more glue-soaked pieces of paper and trim the top to leave a wavy edge. Leave to dry. Finish with a clear coat of diluted PVA glue.

E A R R I N G S   A N D
B R O O C H   S E T

This dazzling set would make a lovely Christmas present – especially in these jewel-like colours! The earring backs, brooch clip and head pins are known as 'findings' and are available from hobby and craft suppliers, as well as theatrical costumiers.

YOU WILL NEED

Heavy corrugated cardboard
Pair of compasses
Pencil
Craft knife
Newspaper
Diluted PVA glue
Fine sandpaper
White and gold acrylic paint
Small paintbrush
Strong clear glue
Glass 'gems' and small beads
Darning needle
9 headpins
Pair of earring backs
Brooch clip

1 Draw two 2.5 cm (1 in) circles and one 5 cm (2 in) circle on heavy cardboard, and cut out with a craft knife.

2 Tear newspaper into strips about 6–12 mm (¼–½ in) wide. Fill a bowl with diluted PVA glue. Dip each strip of paper into the glue, and apply to the brooch and earring pieces. The paper strips should overlap slightly, to add strength to the pieces. Cover each with four layers of papier-mâché. Allow to dry overnight in a warm place.

3 Smooth the jewellery pieces lightly with fine sandpaper, and then prime each with two coats of white paint. When they are dry, decorate with two coats of gold paint.

4 Stick the glass 'gems' to the front of each earring, and the brooch. Make three holes in the bottom of each piece with a darning needle. Fix a hanging bead onto the top of each headpin, dab a spot of glue around each hole, and push the stems of the headpins in place. Stick the brooch clip and earring backs in place with strong clear glue.

VASE

This light, strong vase is not waterproof but an arrangement of dried or artificial flowers would look very striking in it. Other shapes and designs can be created by adapting this idea.

YOU WILL NEED
Heavy corrugated cardboard
Pencil
Craft knife
Plain paper
Masking tape
Clear glue
Diluted PVA glue
Newspaper
White matt emulsion paint
Large paintbrush
Fine sandpaper
Coloured chalk
Small paintbrush
Gouache paints
Clear polyurethane varnish

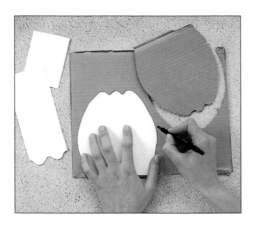

1 Scale up the template and use to cut out the vase shapes from heavy corrugated cardboard.

2 Using masking tape and clear glue, construct the vase leaving the front open. Coat all the pieces with diluted PVA glue to strengthen the vase. Allow these to dry for 3–4 hours. Shred newspaper into strips, and soak in diluted PVA. Cover all the pieces with four layers of papier mâché. Leave to dry in a warm place for about 12 hours. Prime the inside of the vase with two coats of white matt emulsion paint and leave to dry.

3 Use clear glue and masking tape to stick the front onto the vase. Cover the joins with four layers of papier mâché. Leave to dry, then rub down with fine sandpaper. Paint with two coats of matt white emulsion and again leave to dry.

4 Draw a motif onto a piece of paper. Chalk the back of this design using coloured chalk. Place the chalked paper on the front of the vase, securing it with masking tape. Draw over the design with a pencil, then remove the paper carefully. Draw over the chalk imprint lightly with the pencil. Cover the vase with a coloured paint wash. Paint in the shapes using gouache. Leave to dry. Seal with two coats of clear polyurethane varnish.

TRINKET DISH

This trinket dish takes its inspiration from Celtic metalwork. Although the design is simple, it is very effective and bright.

YOU WILL NEED

Bowl to use as a mould
Petroleum jelly
Newspaper
Diluted PVA glue
Scissors
Fine sandpaper
White and gold acrylic paint
Small paintbrush
Glass 'gems'
Strong clear glue

1 Grease the inside of the bowl lightly with petroleum jelly to allow easy removal of the papier-mâché when dry. Tear newspaper into strips about 2.5 cm (1 in) wide. Fill a bowl with diluted PVA glue and dip a strip of paper into it. Lay the glued paper into the greased bowl, and smooth it gently into the curves. Lay a second strip of paper so that it slightly covers the first, and continue until the inside of the bowl is completely covered. Repeat the process until you have completed four layers of papier-mâché, and then leave to dry overnight in a warm place.

2 When the papier-mâché is dry, remove it carefully from the mould. Trim the edges of the paper shape, and bind them with short, narrow strips of newspaper which have been dipped in the bowl of diluted PVA glue. Let the papier-mâché dish dry thoroughly.

3 Smooth the bowl lightly with fine sandpaper, and prime it with two coats of white paint. Apply two coats of gold paint and allow to dry thoroughly.

4 Fix the glass 'gems' to the bowl using strong clear glue. Space the stones evenly, and use a variety of colours.

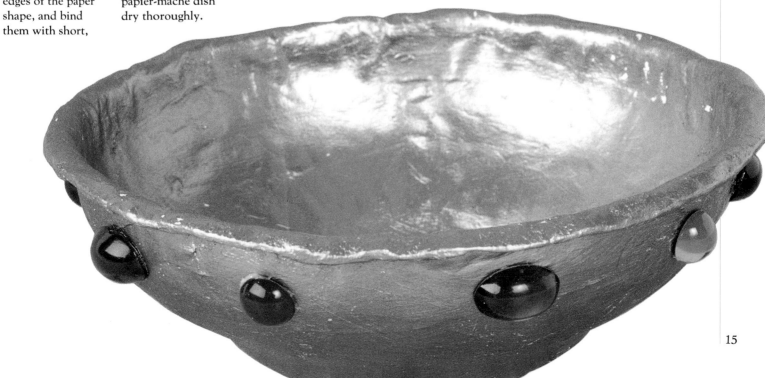

WHIRLING WINDMILL

Small children never cease to be fascinated by a windmill. The ribbon hides the straw as well as being decorative. You can use any combination of colours; try winding two different colours of ribbon around the straw.

YOU WILL NEED
Pencil
Ruler
Square of stiff paper
Scissors
Map pin
Empty ballpoint pen ink cartridge
Plastic drinking straw
Disc of cork
Ribbon

1 Scale up the pattern from the template and transfer it onto a square of stiff paper. Cut along the lines from each corner 7.5 cm (3 in) into the centre. Make a pin hole in alternate points and curl these over to the centre.

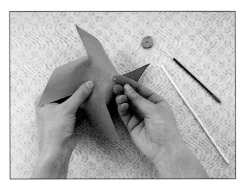

2 Push the map pin through all four points in the centre to the back of the windmill shape.

3 Use a small piece cut from the end of an empty ballpoint pen ink cartridge as a bearing to enable the windmill to turn. Fit it over the point of the pin and then push the pin through a drinking straw. To stop the pin protruding and to secure it, push the point into a disc of cork. Wind a long piece of ribbon up the length of the straw, leaving a gap of about 3 cm (1¼ in) at the top so that the windmill can turn freely. Then wind the ribbon back down to the bottom and finish with a neat knot, leaving a loose piece at the end. Make four small cuts in the loose end to fringe.

BOOK MARK

Are you always losing your place in the book you are reading? Keep track of your place in a favourite book, piece of music or collection of fairy tales with this lively and appealing book mark.

YOU WILL NEED
Pencil
Ruler
Stiff card
Scissors
Assorted acrylic paints
Small paintbrush

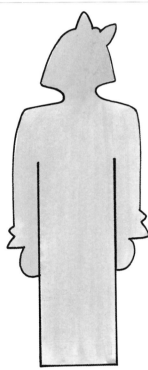

1 Cut out a rectangle about 6 cm × 14 cm (2¼ in × 5½ in) in stiff card using scissors. Scale up the template and transfer it to the card.

2 Draw in the detail and start to paint with acrylic paint, having mixed the colours to a creamy consistency. Allow to dry.

3 Cut out the shape. Cut into the arms, leaving two slits to slot over a page of a book to mark your place.

FLOWER COLLAGE

A collage is a good way of using up all sorts of scrap paper. Before you start, choose a theme. The subject here is a vase of flowers. Scissors are used to make the sharp edges, contrasting with pieces of torn paper for a varied effect. Sugar paper has a nice rough quality and can be easily torn into different shapes.

YOU WILL NEED
Scissors
Coloured paper
Strong clear glue
White card

1 Using scissors, cut up coloured paper for all the sharp edges such as the table top and vase. Tear lots of paper into plant-like shapes such as leaves and flowers.

2 Place the pieces representing the table top and vase onto a large sheet of paper. Then stick them down in sequence with glue.

3 Arrange the flowers and leaves and stick down the shapes with glue. Work in a systematic way, overlapping the shapes. When the design has dried, mount it onto a piece of white card to strengthen the completed collage.

FINGER PUPPETS

This is a fun way to entertain yourself and the children without too much exertion. Have a great time creating the finger puppets and making up a play introducing all your own characters.

YOU WILL NEED
Thin white card
Scissors
Strong clear glue
Coloured gummed paper strips
Crêpe paper
Coloured tissue paper
Black and red felt-tip pens

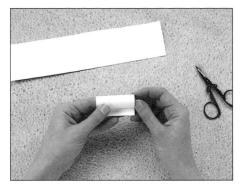

1 Cut out a small rectangular piece of card, wrap it around your finger for size and trim it with scissors, allowing for a slight overlap. Stick down with glue to form a small tube, and hold until stuck.

2 Cut strips of gummed paper to size with scissors. Moisten the back of the gummed paper with water and stick halfway down the small tube to represent clothes.

3 Cut out a narrow strip of card 6 cm (2¼ in) long for the arms and cover with a narrow strip of coloured gummed paper, leaving a little piece of white card showing at both ends for the hands. Curve the centre of the strip around the body, making sure that an equal length of arm is visible either side of the tube. Glue in place halfway down.

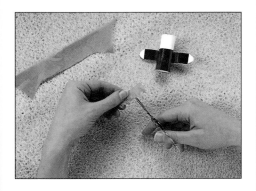

4 For added decoration, fringe a narrow strip of crêpe paper with scissors and stick onto the top edge of the gummed paper with glue.

5 Finally, cut a narrow strip of coloured tissue paper for the hair and fringe with scissors. Then stick in onto the top end of the tube with glue. Draw a face and hands onto the areas which are left white with a black felt-tip pen. Fill in the lips and colour the cheeks with a red felt-tip pen.

STAINED GLASS PICTURE

If you have ever admired stained glass in a church window, and wanted to make some for your own home, here is a simple method using tissue paper instead of glass, and black cartridge paper to emulate leading. You might like to suggest the name of your house in the design, and hang the picture in your front porch, or perhaps make some pretty decorative panels for a guest room or the arrival of a friend.

YOU WILL NEED
Pencil
Plain paper
Black paper
White pencil
Craft knife
Coloured tissue paper
Paper glue
Scissors

1 Design your stained glass picture on some plain paper, and then copy it onto a sheet of black paper with a white pencil. Using a craft knife, cut out the paper inside the white pencil lines to leave a black 'skeleton' framework.

2 Draw around the black framework onto another sheet of black cartridge paper and cut it out.

3 Work out where to place each colour, and then trace off each section of window onto a suitably coloured piece of tissue paper. Cut out the tissue slightly larger for gluing, and stick it to the back of one framework.

4 Stick the second framework to the back of the first, pencil side in. When the frame has dried, suspend the picture in a strong light source to give the impression of stained glass.

SILVER FRAME

This is an easy and cost-effective way of making a fancy frame without any special tools. All you need is some corrugated cardboard and silver baking foil.

YOU WILL NEED
Metal rule
Pencil
Craft knife
Heavy corrugated cardboard
Card
Paper glue
Silver baking foil
Scissors
Picture hanger
Masking tape

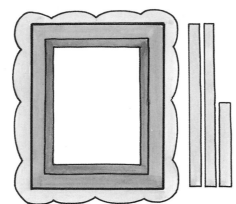

1 Scale up the template to the size required. Using a craft knife and metal rule, cut out all the frame pieces from corrugated cardboard. Again using a craft knife and metal rule, cut out the spacers from card. Then glue together the two smaller borders of the frame.

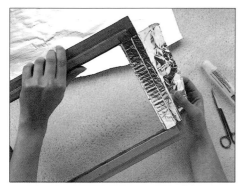

3 Cover the border of the corrugated cardboard with foil. Trim it to size using scissors and glue down. Cover the back piece with foil.

4 Using the point from a pair of scissors, pierce the back piece of the frame at the top, beneath the front border. Insert a picture hanger from the back. Cover the front of the hanger with masking tape.

5 Finally spread glue onto the spacers and stick the front piece of the frame to the back.

2 Glue the three spacers onto the underneath of the front frame. Stick the spacers onto the sides and bottom so that a gap is left at the top to insert a photograph.

PAPER QUILLS

The old-fashioned paper craft known as quilling is used to make this distinctive card. You can design a picture in the same way, and hang it on the wall.

YOU WILL NEED
Assorted coloured papers
Scissors
Strong clear glue
Contrasting coloured card

1 Cut long narrow strips of various shades of coloured paper. First curl one end of each strip with the blunt edge of a pair of scissors, then, starting at this end, roll the strip into a tight coil.

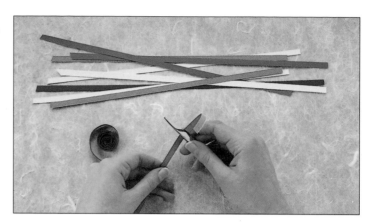

2 Release the coil slightly and glue the end. Hold this in position until the glue is dry. Pinch the outside of the coils between your fingers to form different shapes such as a pear, scroll or eye.

3 Fold a rectangular piece of card in a contrasting colour in half. Arrange the shaped quills on the card and stick down, spreading the glue on the bottom edge of each quill.

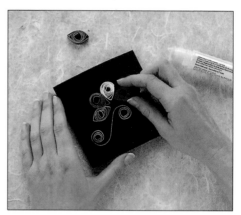

KITCHEN TOOL HOLDER

Turn an empty can into a decorative holder for kitchen tools. Try to find paper that emphasizes some detail in the kitchen, or even paint your own design on plain paper.

YOU WILL NEED
Empty can
White matt emulsion paint
Large paintbrush
Ruler
Pencil
Wrapping paper
Scissors
Strong clear glue
Clear polyurethane varnish

1 Prime the can with white matt emulsion paint. Measure the height and circumference of the can and draw two rectangles on the back of the wrapping paper slightly larger than these measurements, one for the inside of the can and one for the outside. Cut out the pieces. Spread glue on the piece for the inside.

2 Insert this piece inside the can carefully and press it against the walls. Make cuts in the paper projecting at the top of the can so that the paper can be glued down neatly to the outside of the can.

3 Glue the second piece of paper to the outside of the can, making sure the top edge is flush with the rim, and that there is a small overlap at the base. Cut the projecting paper so it can be glued to the bottom.

4 Cut out a circle in the paper, using the can as a guide, and glue this to the base.

5 Cut out a slightly smaller circle in the paper, glue it and lower it into the base of the can. Press into place. Allow to dry. Then apply two coats of clear polyurethane varnish. Allow to dry overnight.

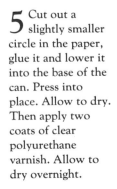

RECYCLED BOX

This 'green' idea should appeal to everyone. Recycle clean old cardboard boxes which perhaps once contained tea bags and cover them with wrapping paper. They make attractive storage boxes for little bits and pieces such as necklaces or bracelets.

YOU WILL NEED
Cardboard box
Metal rule
Patterned and plain wrapping paper
Scissors
Paper glue
Coloured tissue paper

1 Measure all the sides of the box and cut patterned wrapping paper to the approximate size. Wrap the outside of the box with the paper, trim to size with scissors and stick it down with paper glue.

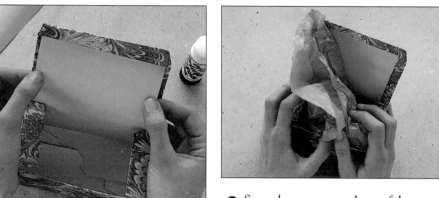

2 Line the inside of the box with plain wrapping paper for neatness.

3 Scrunch up some tissue paper that complements the colours of the wrapping paper and use to line the box.

TISSUE BOX COVERS

This is a novel way to disguise tissue boxes and hide the brand names. Choose a wrapping paper that blends neatly into your colour scheme.

YOU WILL NEED
Tissue box
Metal rule
Thin white card
Pencil
Craft knife
Clear glue
Wrapping paper
Scissors

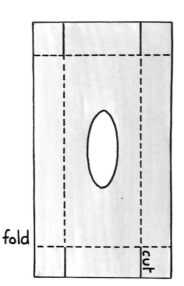

fold

cut

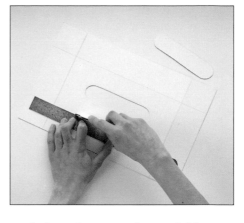

1 Scale up the template to the size required to fit the tissue box, adding 12 mm (½ in) to all the measurements of the original tissue box. Transfer the pattern onto thin white card. Using a craft knife, cut out the pattern. Using a metal rule and craft knife lightly score all the edges that need to be folded. Be careful not to cut right through the card.

2 Fold the top edges and the tabs, and stick the corners together with glue.

3 Using the same template cut out the wrapping paper. Leave an overlap for the hole in the middle. Fold the paper under and cut darts in the paper. Glue underneath.

4 Next stick the wrapping paper onto the white card with clear glue. Slip the cover over the tissue box and pull the tissues through the opening.

GIFT-WRAPPED

Add to the excitement of a special gift by packing it in this effective box. You can make the box any size, scaling the template up or down to fit the contents. Choose card and ribbon in colours to match your gift, if you like. The 'gems' can be bought from most craft suppliers.

YOU WILL NEED
Ruler
Pencil
Square of stiff card
Craft knife
Paper glue
Ribbon
Stapler
Jewel decorations

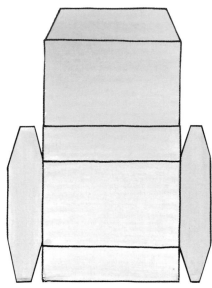

1 Scale up the template to the size required and transfer the measurements onto the card. Cut out the box using a craft knife and ruler. Score along the inside fold of the tabs. Fold the card inwards to make a box. Glue down the tabs onto the inside of the box.

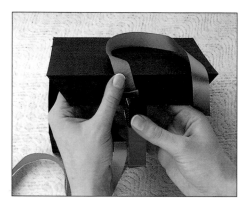

2 Staple one piece of ribbon under the front flap of the box and fold the other piece under the staple onto the front flap of the lid in such a way that the staple does not show when the ribbon is tied.

3 Arrange the 'gems' on the lid in a pretty pattern and glue down. Tie the ribbon in a bow to finish and to hold the box shut.

POP-UP CARD

This jolly cat pops out of a flowery garden and languidly surveys the scene. Use this simple design to make a variety of pop-up cards for different occasions.

YOU WILL NEED

Tracing paper
Pencil
Assortment of coloured cartridge papers
Scissors
Black paint
Small paintbrush
Ruler
Paper glue

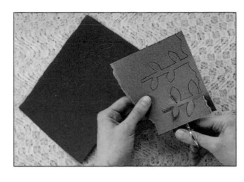

1 Scale up the cat and flower templates. Draw in base tabs. Trace them onto coloured papers and cut out.

2 Paint the details of the cut-outs in black.

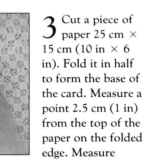

3 Cut a piece of paper 25 cm × 15 cm (10 in × 6 in). Fold it in half to form the base of the card. Measure a point 2.5 cm (1 in) from the top of the paper on the folded edge. Measure another point 4 cm (1½ in) from the folded edge along the top of the card. Draw a diagonal line between these two points. Make a fold inwards along this line, and open out the paper.

4 Fold the cat cut-out in half, and then open it out. Glue the base tabs, and stick the cat along the diagonal lines on the inside of the card.

5 Stick the flowers in position on the inside left of the card.

CHRISTMAS CARD

Black card makes a dramatic background for the angel on this stylish handmade Christmas greeting. Try making a series of different designs on a similar theme.

YOU WILL NEED
Stiff card
Scissors
Image from old card or wrapping paper
Paper glue
Silver glitter pen
Gold self-adhesive stars

1 Cut the card to the size you require and fold it in half. Score along the inside of the fold to make a sharp, neat edge. Cut out an image and glue onto the centre of the card.

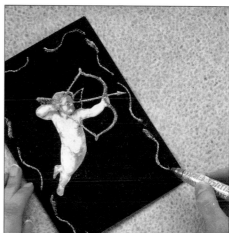

2 Draw some elegant lines with a silver glitter pen around the edge of the card, and allow to dry.

3 Arrange a cluster of gold stars around the central image and a line of them spaced evenly on top of the silver lines to create a border.

DECORATING PAPER

It is fun to design your own wrapping paper. This rustic paper with its oak leaf motif could be used to wrap a woolly sweater in earthy colours, or perhaps some gardening tools. You could even print a friend's name with rubber stamps in the form of letters, or perhaps your own special message.

YOU WILL NEED
Pencil
Erasers
Craft knife
Assorted poster paints, or ink pads
Small paintbrush
Assorted wrapping papers

1 Draw a simple design onto an eraser and cut around it with a craft knife, taking great care to avoid your fingers.

2 Apply a coat of paint to the image on your rubber stamp, and press the stamp down firmly onto the wrapping paper. Take care not to make the paint too runny, as it would spread and blur the image. Alternatively, press the stamp onto an ink pad.

3 A more delicate effect is achieved by printing on white tissue paper, which would be particularly suitable for wrapping wedding or christening gifts.

GIFT TAGS

Why buy expensive gift tags when you can make your own from scraps of paper? Match or contrast the tags with the wrapping paper, or make plain ones and decorate them with sequins, scraps of felt, coloured foil or glitter.

1 Cut a 10 cm × 5 cm (4 in × 2 in) piece of coloured paper. Fold it in half.

YOU WILL NEED
Ruler
Scraps of coloured paper
Scissors
Pencil
Paper glue
Hole punch
Thin string

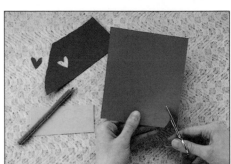

2 Draw hearts and wavy lines onto contrasting pieces of coloured paper and cut them out.

3 Stick them in place with paper glue.

4 Punch a hole on the inside top left-hand corner of the gift tag. Thread a length of thin string through the hole.

STATIONERY SET

Co-ordinated stationery looks very attractive — you might like to make a complete set for all your correspondence, including invitation cards. You could choose a simple motif such as a star or heart, or perhaps your initials or a monogram. You could also make this stationery wallet to keep everything together.

YOU WILL NEED
Pencil
Scraps of paper in contrasting colours
Sheets of writing paper and envelopes
Scissors
Paper glue
*Piece of thin card in complementary
    colour*

1 Draw your design onto paper that contrasts with or complements the colour of your writing paper. Cut out each element of the design.

2 Place the cut-outs on the stationery and stick in position. You might prefer the top left-hand corner, or perhaps the top centre of each sheet of paper. The back or front of each envelope may be decorated similarly.

3 Cut out a stationery wallet in thin card to hold the paper. The wallet may be decorated in the same way as the stationery.

PLACE CARDS

Place cards can set the mood for a meal. Perhaps you want to convey a sophisticated atmosphere with very plain cards, or a jazzy, fun air with bright, vivid colours and clever cut-outs. You can also follow the theme of the occasion such as a birthday or anniversary celebration.

YOU WILL NEED
Paper in a variety of colours
Scraps of paper in contrasting colours
Pencil
Scissors
Paper glue
Black felt-tip pen

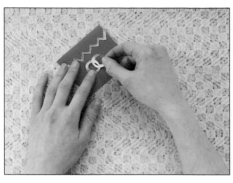

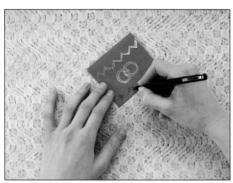

1 Cut a small rectangle of cartridge paper. Draw your chosen design onto contrasting paper and cut it out.

2 Fold a small piece of coloured paper in half to form the place card. Position each element of the design, and stick it in place.

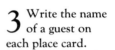

3 Write the name of a guest on each place card.

CHRISTMAS CRACKER

Decorate your Christmas tree with lots of fancy crackers. Fill them with tiny gifts and pull them during the festive season.

YOU WILL NEED
Cardboard tube
Silver doily
Scissors
Crêpe paper
Strong clear glue
Ribbon
Foil ribbon

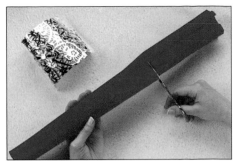

1 Place the cardboard tube on top of the silver doily and trim the doily to size using scissors.

2 Place the cardboard tube on a length of crêpe paper which will cover the whole tube. Trim the ends, leaving at least 10 cm (4 in) at both ends. Glue the crêpe paper where the seam is formed. Next place the silver doily on top of the tube and glue down.

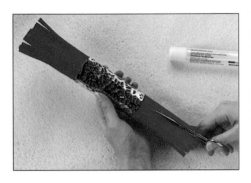

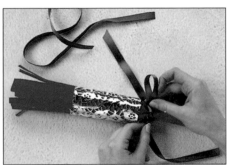

3 When this is secure, fringe the ends of the crêpe paper. This is done by cutting into the ends with scissors at regular intervals all around the circumference.

4 Next cut two lengths of ribbon about 30 cm (12 in) long and tie a bow at both ends of the cracker.

5 Pull long strips of the foil ribbon through closed scissors to make it twist and curl into ringlets. Tie onto both ends of the cracker.

FLOWER GARLAND

Festoon a ceiling and walls with festive flower garlands made of coloured tissue paper. Use bright colours for the flowers, and green for the leaves.

3 Fold the shapes in half so that you can cut a hole neatly in the centre, using the scissors.

YOU WILL NEED
Coloured tissue paper
Thin card
Black felt-tip pen
Scissors
Paper glue
Coloured string

4 For each flower, glue the centre of a brightly coloured shape and place directly on top of another shape of the same coloured tissue paper. Press down firmly.

1 Fold sheets of tissue paper so that a number of shapes can be cut simultaneously. Scale up the flower shape on the template onto card and draw around it with a black pen onto the folded sheets of tissue.

2 Cut out the flower shape with scissors, keeping the layers together. Repeat this until you have enough shapes of different colours.

5 The leaves are formed in the same way as the flowers, by gluing in the centre. To join the flowers and leaves, glue the tips of three petals on one side of a flower shape and place a green shape on top. Continue sticking the shapes alternately at the tips and centre. Alternate leaves and flowers until the garland is built up.

6 Finally, thread a piece of coloured string through the central holes to hang the garland.

LAMPSHADE

Dress up that jaded shade by covering it with wrapping paper or wallpaper. The design or colours of the shade can be chosen to co-ordinate with the furnishing scheme of your room.

YOU WILL NEED
Lampshade
Brown parcel paper
Wrapping paper or wallpaper
Pencil
Craft knife
Coin
Scissors
Clear glue
Masking tape
Clear polyurethane varnish
Large paintbrush

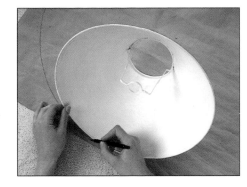

1 Lay the lampshade on its side on the brown parcel paper and slowly rotate it, drawing the shape as you go along to achieve the correct measurement. Use this shape as the template for the lampshade.

2 Cut out the brown parcel paper shape slightly outside the drawn line using a craft knife. Draw a scalloped edge using a coin as a template and cut out scallops.

3 Place the template onto the wrong side of the wrapping paper and secure with masking tape. Then draw around the template and cut out this shape.

4 Spread glue onto the lampshade and stick down the paper slowly, smoothing out any bumps or air pockets as you go round.

5 Make cuts in the protruding paper at the top so that it can be glued down neatly to the inside of the frame. Apply two coats of clear polyurethane varnish so that the lampshade may be wiped clean.

GIFT BOXES

Presents always seem more intriguing if packed in a special box — here are two that have been decorated with holly leaves for Christmas and flowers for spring. Other suitable motifs include Christmas trees, angels and reindeer.

1 Using a pencil, draw your designs onto coloured paper.

YOU WILL NEED
Assortment of coloured paper or old
*   catalogues*
Pencil
Scissors
Gift boxes
Paper glue

2 Cut them out carefully using scissors.

3 Arrange the cut-outs on the gift box and stick them in position with paper glue.

4 As an alternative, cover a plain gold gift box with photographs of flowers cut out of a seed catalogue.

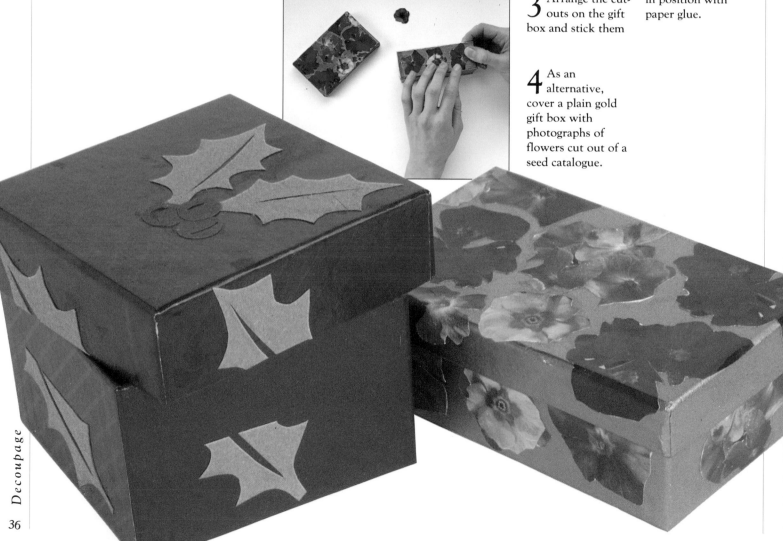

MODEL CLOCK

This highly original timepiece would delight any collector of bizarre objects! The figure is typical of the models daringly featured in Victorian mail-order catalogues.

YOU WILL NEED
Drill
Piece of plywood
Paper images from old magazines
Scissors
Diluted PVA glue
Pencil
Dark oak-coloured varnish
Small paintbrush
Soft cloth
Clear matt varnish
Clock mechanism
Clock hands
Battery

1 Drill a hole, large enough for a clock mechanism, in a primed piece of plywood. Cut out suitable paper images and clock face and arrange on the piece of plywood.

2 Make sure that the centre of the clock face is directly above the drilled hole. Stick the design in position using diluted PVA glue. Rub the paper with your hands until it is smooth. Using a pencil, pierce a hole in the centre of the clock face.

3 Allow 1 hour for the glue to dry, then apply dark oak-coloured varnish with a small paintbrush. Before it dries, rub it off in circular movements with a soft cloth, working from the centre outwards. Leave to dry.

4 Apply a coat of clear matt varnish. When this is dry, fit the clock mechanism and connect the hands to the front. Insert the battery.

WASTE PAPER BASKET

Decoupage decoration quickly covers surfaces in beautiful and unusual designs. It is particularly effective on shiny materials, such as this metal waste paper basket.

YOU WILL NEED
Flat brush
Diluted PVA glue
Metal waste paper basket
Pale blue and yellow tissue paper
Scissors
Flowery wrapping paper
Clear polyurethane varnish

1 Brush PVA glue liberally all over the waste paper basket.

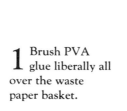

2 Tear long strips of tissue paper and paste them round the middle area of the basket.

3 Cut out an assortment of strips and pretty motifs from wrapping paper.

4 Decide on the design of the basket and dip the pieces of wrapping paper in PVA glue. Stick them onto the basket according to your chosen design, brushing them flat as you work. Add more strips of tissue paper until the design is complete. Leave to dry. Finish with a final coat of glue and leave to dry. Cover with a coat of clear polyurethane varnish and leave to dry.

HAT BOX

This traditional hat box can be used to store a variety of objects other than hats. It is also an attractive piece to display in your home. A simple form of decoupage using wrapping paper is shown here. You can of course cut out pictures from magazines, old postcards and greeting cards, building up layers of images.

YOU WILL NEED
Hat box
White matt emulsion paint
Large paintbrush
Fine sandpaper
Piece of natural sponge
Poster paint
Rag
Wrapping paper
Scissors
Diluted PVA glue
Coloured varnish

1 Paint the hat box with matt white emulsion paint. Rub down using fine sandpaper. Using a piece of natural sponge, add a wash of watery paint to age the box, removing some of the paint with a rag as you go.

2 Choose a paper with an attractive design and cut out the images that most appeal to you. Arrange the paper on the box ready to glue on.

3 Glue your images onto the box using diluted PVA glue and leave to dry.

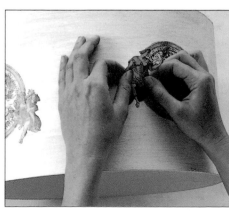

4 Varnish the box with a coloured varnish, again removing a lot of it with a rag to give the box warmth and to add to its antiqued look.

SHOE BOX

The pictures of shoes decorating this box have been dipped in cold tea to antique them. This technique is very effective, and a variety of different images could be used. For example, pictures of hats could adorn a circular hat box, or jewels a trinket box. Good sources of illustrations are old clothing catalogues, greetings cards, and any Victorian or Edwardian technical manuals.

YOU WILL NEED
Brown wrapping paper
Cardboard shoe box
Scissors
Paper glue
Old shoe catalogues
Cold tea

1 Cut out pieces of brown wrapping paper to fit a cardboard shoe box. Use to cover the box and lid completely and glue in place.

2 Roughly cut out the chosen images from the catalogues. Fill a small bowl with cold tea, and submerge each image for a few seconds so that the tea penetrates the paper. Pin each image up to dry. If the images hang vertically, this should prevent them from wrinkling as they dry. If they do become a little creased, press them quickly on the reverse using a cool iron.

3 Cut around the pictures carefully with small scissors and arrange them on the box and lid.

4 When you are satisfied with your design, stick each picture in position.

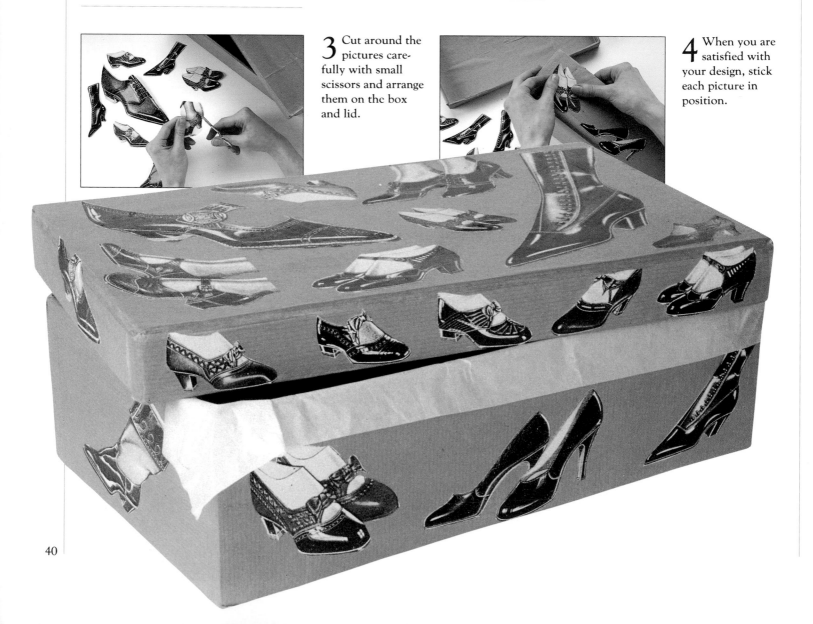

HAND MIRROR

Decorate a dull hand mirror with ornate decoupage motifs to add a beautiful touch to the dressing table. You could even make a matching set with a decorated hairbrush and other toilet items.

YOU WILL NEED
Plastic hand mirror
Fine sandpaper
Plain paper
Masking tape
Scissors
Poster paint in a complementary colour
Small paintbrush
Wrapping paper
Diluted PVA glue

1 Lightly sand the plain surfaces of the mirror using fine sandpaper.

2 Cut out a plain paper shield to fit over the mirror glass and stick in place with masking tape.

3 Paint the plastic surfaces with poster paint, allowing each coat to dry thoroughly.

4 Cut out motifs from wrapping paper and arrange over the handle and back of the mirror. Dip each piece into diluted PVA, place on the mirror and brush more glue on top.

5 Using small strips of wrapping paper, decorate the rim and front edge in the same way. Leave to dry overnight. Remove the paper and tape from the front edge.

CAKE TIN

This metal cake tin has been given a new lease of life with some white paint and jazzy tartlet motifs — you could, of course, depict any type of confectionery you wanted!

YOU WILL NEED
Metal cake tin
White poster paint
Paintbrush
Pencil
Coloured cartridge paper
Scissors
Paper glue
Clear gloss varnish

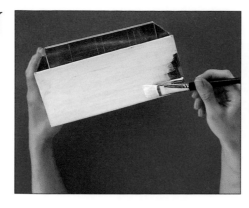

1 Wash the cake tin to remove any grease and then prime the outside with a coat of white paint. Leave to dry, then apply a second coat to give a good dense base colour.

2 Draw your designs onto cartridge paper and cut them out.

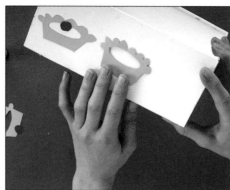

3 Arrange the cut-outs on the sides and lid of the tin. Stick them in position with glue.

4 Seal the tin with two coats of varnish. Allow to dry thoroughly before you use the tin.

PRIVATE LETTER BOX

This ornate box can be used to store those secret letters, or to keep documents safe. Use brightly coloured wrapping paper to decorate it, saving oddments for extra details.

YOU WILL NEED
Thin cardboard
Scissors
Craft knife
Metal rule
Strong clear glue
Masking tape
Wrapping paper
Large paintbrush
Diluted PVA glue
Narrow ribbon
Button

2 Strengthen the edges of the box with strips of masking tape.

1 Scale up the template to the size required and transfer to a piece of thin cardboard. Cut out the box shape. Score along the folds using a craft knife and metal rule. Fold in the tabs and glue firmly in place along the sides.

3 Cut out motifs from wrapping paper and decide where to position them on the box. Stick down with diluted PVA glue, brushing an extra coat of glue over the pieces to varnish them. Allow to dry. Fix a loop of ribbon under the flap of the lid and a button on the front of the box to fasten.

CUPID CUPBOARD

If you see a shabby old cupboard in an auction sale, why not bid for it? Decoupage is an easy way to turn such a piece of furniture into a charming addition to your home, and you do not need to have any special artistic skills.

YOU WILL NEED
Scissors
Decorative paper images
Small cupboard
Medium sandpaper
White spirit
White matt emulsion paint
Diluted wood glue
Small paintbrush
Acrylic varnish
Large paintbrush
Antique oak-coloured varnish
Soft cloth

1 Using scissors, cut out the decorative images required for the decoupage.

2 To prepare the cupboard, rub down with sandpaper, clean with white spirit and coat twice with white matt emulsion paint. Arrange the cut-out images on the cupboard and stick down with diluted wood glue. Make sure the glue is spread evenly over the images. Leave to dry for 1 hour.

3 Using a small paintbrush, apply a coat of acrylic varnish to the decoupage images only. This will protect them against the next stage of varnishing. Allow the acrylic varnish to dry for 30 minutes.

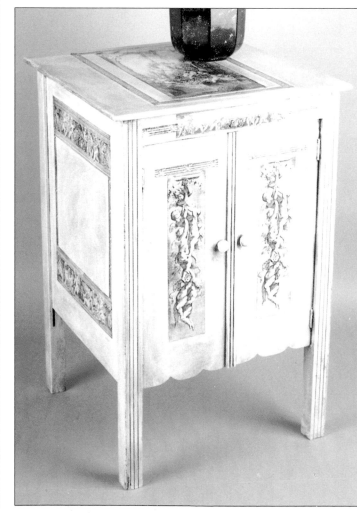

4 Using a large paintbrush, apply the antique oak-coloured varnish to small areas at a time. As soon as you have brushed on the varnish, wipe it off quickly with a soft cloth. Repeat this process until the whole cupboard has been varnished. This stains the white painted areas while the oak-coloured varnish stays intact in cracks and grooves.

MOSAIC TRAY

Create a useful and evocative souvenir of your travels with a collection of postcards. Select a variety of pictures that capture your memories, or those of a friend or relative, and use to transform an old tray into a piece of art.

YOU WILL NEED
Old tray
Sandpaper
White matt emulsion paint
PVA glue
Blue poster paint
Large paintbrush
Scissors
Assorted picture postcards

1 Clean and lightly sand the tray. Prime with one coat of white emulsion. Leave to dry. Mix two tablespoons of PVA glue with the blue poster paint and apply one coat to the tray. Leave to dry. Cut up picture postcards into triangles.

2 Decide on the arrangement of the images on the tray. Mix ¾ cup PVA to ¼ cup water. Dip each triangle into the glue and position on the tray, turning the tray as you work. Add small strips cut from postcards along the top edges of the tray. When the design is complete, varnish the tray with two coats of PVA glue.

IVY
MIRROR

'Mirror, mirror on the wall — who is the fairest of them all?' By painting a trail of ivy on the frame, this mirror becomes a decorative feature for a country bedroom. Experiment using alternative designs made up of flowers or intricately-shaped leaves.

YOU WILL NEED
Wooden-framed mirror
Masking tape
White matt emulsion paint
Large paintbrush
Paper
Pencil
Carbon paper
Small paintbrush
Green and white acrylic paint
Soft cloths
Finishing wax

1 Prepare the mirror. Put strips of masking tape all round the edges of the mirror close to the frame to prevent paint from getting onto the mirror. Apply two coats of white matt emulsion paint.

2 Draw an ivy design onto paper to fit the mirror. Place a strip of carbon paper face down on the mirror frame and secure with masking tape. Lay the ivy design on top and secure in the same way. Draw around the design with a pencil so it is reproduced on the frame in carbon. Repeat this process until the whole design is copied onto the frame.

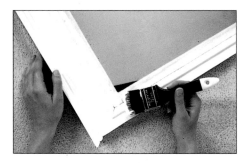

3 Using a small paintbrush, paint the meandering ivy with a mixture of green and white acrylic paint.

4 Use a darker mixture of green to paint an outline and other details. Using a soft cloth, polish the mirror frame with two coats of finishing wax. Allow each coat to dry and polish again.

5 When the wax is dry, remove the masking tape to reveal a clean mirror.

PAINTED BUCKET

This bucket is influenced by the canal boat painters and uses their traditional colours of green, red and yellow.

YOU WILL NEED
Metal bucket
Wire (steel) wool
Green, red, yellow and black enamel paint
Large paintbrush
Pencil
Tracing paper
White paper
Chalk
Masking tape
Small paintbrush

1 Rub down the bucket with wire wool. Paint it with two coats of green enamel paint using a large paintbrush. Scale up the template to fit your bucket, tracing the design onto paper. Rub chalk onto the back of the template and attach to the bucket side with masking tape. Draw the design on top with a pencil and the image will be duplicated in chalk.

2 Remove the template carefully so as not to disturb the chalk. Paint the areas of red and yellow using a small brush. Apply two coats and allow to dry for 6 hours between each coat.

3 When all the colours are dry, finish off by adding black outlines and details with a small paintbrush. Allow the paint to dry forming a tough coat. Varnish is not necessary for this piece.

TOY CHEST

This colourful chest can be used in a child's room for storing toys and puzzles. Try to think of as many different colours as you can for the kites and bows — experiment with mixing your own shades.

YOU WILL NEED
Toy chest
White matt emulsion paint
Large paintbrush
Sandpaper
White chalk
Stiff black card
Scissors
Pencil
Assorted acrylic paints
Small paintbrush
Masking tape
Clear satin polyurethane varnish

1 Prepare the chest. Paint it white, leave to dry and rub down with sandpaper. Apply a second coat of white paint and leave to dry. Scale up and draw the shape of the kite and bows with white chalk on black card and cut them out. Hold the templates against the chest and move them around until you have arranged them satisfactorily. Then draw around each template with a pencil. Draw in the detail and link up the bows and kites with a flowing pencil line.

2 Using a small paintbrush, paint the edges of the chest in blue acrylic paint, covering the borders with masking tape to give a neat line.

3 Start painting in the design. You may need to give it a couple of coats to achieve an even finish. Using a small paintbrush in a confident manner, link up the bows following your flowing pencil line with burnt umber acrylic paints. Add the finishing touches with a paler tone of each colour to add movement and dimension. Allow to dry. Apply polyurethane varnish, giving the chest at least two coats for maximum protection. Leave to dry overnight.

FOOT STOOL

The red tulips and blue decoration on this stool are reminiscent of early American folk art. This idea can be adapted to transform any piece of secondhand furniture.

YOU WILL NEED
Stool
Sandpaper
White matt emulsion paint
Metal rule
Plain paper
Pencil
Scissors
Coloured chalk
Masking tape
Soft cloth
Assorted gouache paints
Small paintbrush
Gloss polyurethane varnish

1 Rub down the stool with sandpaper and paint with matt white emulsion paint. Measure the surfaces to be decorated, then draw the planned design onto paper. Cut out to size. Completely cover the back of the paper with chalk. Hold it in place on the stool with masking tape. Draw over the design firmly with pencil, and remove the drawing paper. Follow the chalk design carefully and lightly with pencil, and wipe off the loose chalk with a soft cloth.

2 Paint on the design with gouache paints using a small paintbrush. Leave to dry. Then seal the stool with two coats of gloss polyurethane varnish.

SIDE TABLE

You might find an old piece of furniture that has a pleasing shape or line but is in terrible condition. Strip off any old paint and start again. This is a very simple linear design painted on just such a 'rescued' table. Masking tape is invaluable for helping to paint straight lines.

YOU WILL NEED
Table
White matt emulsion paint
Large paintbrush
Yellow ochre and raw umber acrylic
*   paints*
Ruler
Pencil
Masking tape
Small paintbrush
Antique pine-coloured varnish
Soft cloth
Matt varnish

1 Prepare the table. Apply two coats of white matt emulsion. For the base cream colour, mix yellow ochre acrylic paint and white matt emulsion paint. Apply two coats. Measure and mark out the linear design on the table with a pencil. Using the markings as a guide, lay down long parallel strips of masking tape to protect the areas not to be painted.

2 Using a small paintbrush, fill in the exposed areas. This design starts with a dark tone which gets gradually lighter. To achieve this, mix raw umber acrylic paint and white matt emulsion paint in the required proportions. Allow to dry for 30 minutes.

3 When the paint is completely dry, peel off all the masking tape carefully. A little re-touching may be needed at this point.

4 Next, brush on the antique pine-coloured varnish with a large paintbrush, working in small areas at a time, and rub it off immed-iately with a soft cloth. Repeat this until the whole table has been covered to give it a nice warm tone. Finally, give the table a coat of matt varnish with a large paintbrush, in a well-ventilated room.

WICKER BASKET

Here an ordinary wicker basket is given a new lease of life for a baby's room. When choosing a basket, look out for little details which you can emphasize to give it that personal touch.

YOU WILL NEED
Wicker basket
White matt emulsion paint
Large paintbrush
Blue and red acrylic paint
Small paintbrush

1 First paint the inside and outside of the wicker basket with white matt emulsion paint, using a large paintbrush.

2 When the white paint is dry, mix a little blue acrylic paint with some white matt emulsion paint to make a baby blue. Also mix a little red acrylic paint with some white matt emulsion to make a baby pink. Using a small paintbrush, pick out the detail on the wicker basket in contrasting colours.

DESIGNER SHELVES

These pretty shelves are in the tradition of tole painting. You can make them to any size or renovate old or existing shelving. Choose colours to match the room; a combination of blue and white is both simple and effective. Practise the brush strokes on a piece of paper before you start, to gain enough confidence to achieve the design.

YOU WILL NEED
Shelves
White matt emulsion paint
Large paintbrush
Fine sandpaper
Pencil
Blue acrylic paint
Small paintbrush
Clear polyurethane varnish

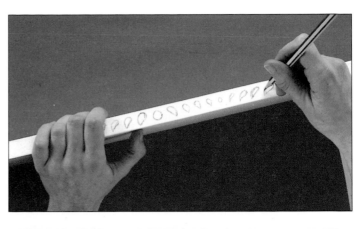

1 Prime the shelves with white emulsion paint and rub down with fine sandpaper. Pencil on the design.

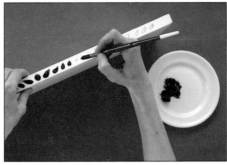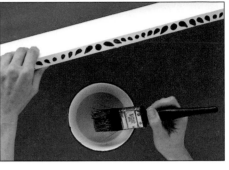

2 Mix the blue acrylic paint to a creamy consistency. Paint the design gently but precisely using single confident brush strokes.

3 Varnish the finished shelves with clear polyurethane varnish to protect the design and so that they may be wiped clean.

HOOK BOARD

Brighten up your hallway by painting a simple bow motif to join coat hooks on an old length of board, and attach it to the wall.

YOU WILL NEED
Length of board with coat hooks
Medium sandpaper
White spirit
Soft cloth
White matt emulsion paint
Large paintbrush
Assorted acrylic paints
Pencil
Small paintbrush
Metallic gold paint
Clear gloss varnish

1 Sand the length of board until it is smooth. Then wipe the surface with white spirit and a soft cloth.

2 Apply a coat of white matt emulsion paint with a large paintbrush. Leave for 30 minutes to dry.

3 Mix up a buttermilk colour with a little yellow ochre acrylic paint and some white matt emulsion paint. Apply two coats, avoiding the hooks.

4 Then draw a bow motif onto the board using a pencil. Fill in the design with red acrylic paint using a small paintbrush. Leave for 10 minutes to dry.

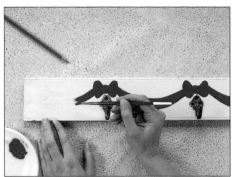

5 Using a small paintbrush, make little strokes to suggest highlights with a mixture of red acrylic and white matt emulsion paint, and shadows with a mixture of red and raw umber acrylic paint. Allow to dry.

6 Then using a small paintbrush, paint the metal hooks with metallic gold paint.

7 Finally, when all the paint is dry, apply a coat of clear gloss varnish, working in a well-ventilated room.

KITCHEN CHAIR

Here the technique of distressing is used. The yellow underneath the top coat of paint shows through on the finished chair as if the colour had worn away with time. On this piece, less traditional colours have been used. The colours you use on your chair can of course complement those in your kitchen.

YOU WILL NEED
Kitchen chair
White matt emulsion paint
Yellow and blue vinyl matt emulsion paint
Large paintbrush
Soft cloth
Beeswax
Medium sandpaper
Pencil
White paper
White chalk
Masking tape
Small paintbrush
Diluted blue acrylic paint

1 Prepare the chair. Prime it with two coats of white matt emulsion paint, then apply two coats of yellow vinyl matt emulsion paint using a large paintbrush. Allow to dry for 2 hours.

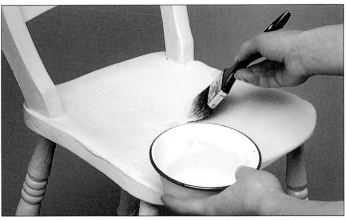

2 Using a cloth, apply a liberal layer of beeswax on the areas where the chair would normally become worn, such as the edges and the seat. Leave to dry for 2 hours.

3 Then apply one coat of blue vinyl matt emulsion paint with a large paintbrush. Leave for 1 hour or until the chair is completely dry.

4 Next, using a piece of medium sandpaper, rub down the entire chair, concentrating particularly on the areas where the beeswax was applied. This will expose patches of the yellow under-coat. Remove all dust with a soft dry cloth before the next step.

5 Using the template, scale up the flower pattern separately on two pieces of paper as necessary to fit on the back of the chair. Cover the reverse of the paper with white chalk and attach each to one bar of the chair with masking tape. Pencil over the design so that the chalk is transferred onto the chair.

6 Using a small paintbrush, fill in the areas of the design with diluted blue acrylic paint. The paint sits lightly on the wax and has a faint textured effect when dry.

7 To finish off the piece and to protect it, apply two layers of beeswax, allowing 1 hour to dry between coats.

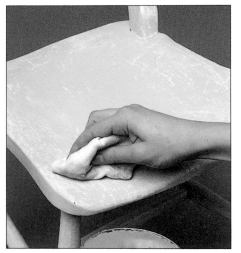

BEDSIDE CUPBOARD

A fleur-de-lys is always an elegant motif and looks most impressive gilded, as on this bedside cupboard.

YOU WILL NEED
Bedside cupboard
White matt emulsion paint
Large paintbrush
Paper
Pencil
Green acrylic paint
Sponge
Gold pigment
Acrylic varnish
Small paintbrush
Clear gloss varnish

1 Prepare the cupboard. Apply two coats of white matt emulsion paint. Scale up and cut out the fleur-de-lys motif template.

Place the template on the top of the cupboard and draw around it using a pencil. Repeat this process on the door.

2 Mix a base colour that is a mid-tone with a mixture of green acrylic and white matt emulsion paint. Cover the whole piece of furniture using a large paintbrush. Paint carefully around the fleur-de-lys motif so that it remains white. Leave this to dry for 1 hour.

3 Mix a darker shade of green, using more green acrylic and less white matt emulsion paint. Place a small quantity of paint on a dish so that it can be spread out thinly. To keep the fleur-de-lys motif white, cover it with the original template. Sponge the darker green up to the edge and onto the paper. Work quickly and lightly all over the cupboard to ensure that there is an even pattern and texture.

4 While the green is drying, mix the gold pigment and acrylic varnish to form a liquid gold. Then paint the fleur-de-lys using a small paintbrush. It may need two coats to ensure it is covered completely.

5 When the gold is dry, paint a shadow and further detail on the fleur-de-lys in a dark green acrylic colour with a small paintbrush. Allow 30 minutes for the paint to dry completely.

6 Then apply a coat of clear gloss varnish using a large paintbrush.

CUP AND SAUCER

The appeal of the bold design on this cup and saucer is its look of spontaneity. If you do not feel confident enough to copy the fluent brush strokes, practise on a piece of broken china. Unless you are absolutely certain that the paints you are using are food-safe, adapt the design by stopping the decoration at least 4 cm (1½ in) below the rim of the cup.

YOU WILL NEED
Non-toxic ceramic enamels
Small paintbrush
White spirit
White china cup and saucer

1 Dip the brush in green ceramic enamel and make bold squiggles on the cup. Leave to dry. Clean the brush before changing colours using white spirit. Between the green shapes paint purple squiggles. Leave to dry.

2 Decorate other white spaces with red ceramic paint. Paint red dots on the handle. Decorate the saucer in the same way.

FEEDING TIME

It is not easy to find attractive bowls for pets, so why not decorate a brightly coloured one with cold enamels? You might like to write your pet's name on the bowl too, to personalize it. Make absolutely certain that you use non-toxic enamels, and only paint the outside of the bowl, *not* the inside.

YOU WILL NEED
China bowl
600 ml (1 pt) warm water with 10 ml (2 tsp) vinegar
Chinagraph pencil
Cold ceramic enamel
Small paintbrush

1 Wash the bowl in the vinegar solution to remove any grease. Dry thoroughly. Draw your design directly onto the bowl with a chinagraph pencil.

2 Paint around the design with enamel colour.

3 Paint a row of fine spots around the outside edge of the bowl.

THAT'S TORN IT

This is a very easy way of giving an inexpensive china mug a distinctive design. You can also decorate a plate to match. Make absolutely sure the ceramic enamels are non-toxic.

YOU WILL NEED
Tape measure
China mug
Masking tape
Scissors
Non-toxic ceramic enamels
Small paintbrush

1 Measure the circumference of the mug and cut three strips of masking tape. Rip the masking tape in half lengthways and place it with the straight edges back to back round the mug in bands.

2 Press the masking tape down so that the paint can not seep under the edges. Apply ceramic enamel to the white areas. Leave to dry overnight.

3 Peel off the masking tape.

WARNING
Take care with the selection of paints. Not all ceramic paints and enamel paints are non-toxic or food-safe. Always study the manufacturer's instructions carefully and follow them exactly. If you have the slightest doubt , NEVER paint any surface that will come into contact with food or the lips or mouth. To adapt a design such as this you would stop the decoration at least 4 cm (1½ in) below the rim of the cup.

TERRACOTTA PLANTER

Brighten up a plant collection with a set of unusually decorated terracotta flowerpots. The clay absorbs some of the colour to create an attractive matt effect. Try experimenting with patterns and colours to create a whole range of designs.

YOU WILL NEED
Terracotta flowerpot
Pencil
Tape measure
Small paintbrush
Assorted ceramic enamels

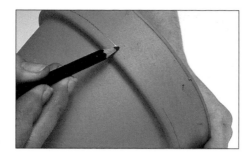

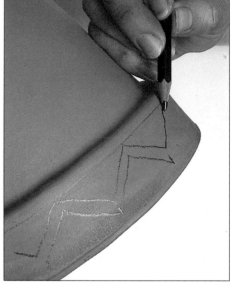

1 Using a pencil, draw two parallel horizontal lines around the top and bottom of the rim of the flowerpot. Keep the lines as straight as possible.

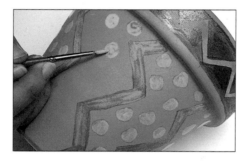

3 Using a small paintbrush, paint the zigzags in one colour and the surrounding area of the rim in a contrasting shade. Mark in vertical zigzags in pencil on the side of the flowerpot and paint in. Paint dots inbetween. Leave to dry.

2 Calculate the circumference of the rim with a tape measure and divide it into an uneven number of equal sections, marking each one with a small pencil mark. Join the marks with two parallel zigzag lines.

FANCY TILES

Why not brighten up your bathroom with the minimum of fuss by decorating the tiles? If you use cold enamels that set without heating, you can paint tiles that are already in place — just remember to follow the manufacturer's instructions, and let the tiles dry thoroughly before you take a bath or shower!

YOU WILL NEED
Ceramic tiles
600 ml (1 pt) warm water with 10 ml (2 tsp) vinegar
Chinagraph pencil
Cold ceramic enamels in a variety of colours
Paintbrushes in various sizes
Tile adhesive and grout (optional)

1 Wash the tiles down with the vinegar solution to remove any grease. Dry thoroughly. Draw your design directly onto the tiles in chinagraph pencil. Any mistakes can be easily removed with a piece of paper or your fingers.

2 Start to fill in the largest area of your design with enamel, using a fairly thick brush. Work quite loosely, as you can add fine details when the first coat of enamel is dry.

3 Add definition to your design by painting on top of the first colour with a darker-toned enamel.

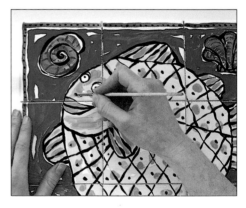

4 If you want a bold effect, outline your design with black enamel. If you are painting loose tiles, stick them in position with tile adhesive. When the adhesive is thoroughly dry add the grouting. Do not allow the tiles to come into contact with water for at least 48 hours.

CANAL BOAT MUG

This colourful mug would make a perfect gift for any canal boat enthusiast. The stylized form of decoration is a traditional feature not only of the boats, but also of buckets and other utensils.

YOU WILL NEED
Small paintbrush
Ceramic enamels
Enamel mug
White spirit

1 Dip the brush in ceramic paint and paint circular shapes onto the mug as a background for the roses. Leave to dry.

Clean the brush before changing colours using white spirit. Paint circles in other colours to form a design.

2 Paint petals on the roses and turn some of the shapes into leaves. Emphasize the detail with black or white ceramic enamels.

3 Outline the design with red dots and paint a

wavy red line on the handle.

CHRISTMAS CANDLE HOLDERS

Why not create decorative candle holders especially for the festive season? Green holly leaves and red berries are quite easy to paint directly onto the china, using a sprig of fresh holly as a pattern.

YOU WILL NEED
Plain white candle holder
Red and green ceramic enamels
Small paint brush
White spirit (paint thinner)

1 Paint outlines of the holly leaves in green ceramic enamel all round the candle holder, then fill in each leaf in the same colour. Leave to dry.

2 Clean the brush before changing colours using white spirit. Paint red berries between the leaves.

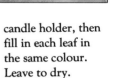

PLANT POT IN RELIEF

Many pieces of china are available with patterns that are raised or 'in relief'. The detail can be further emphasized by colouring the design in ceramic paint, perhaps in the shades suggested by the patterns on the china or even to match a particular interior decor scheme. Cold ceramic enamels are easy to apply but it is best to avoid painting china used for food.

YOU WILL NEED
China pot with relief design
Cold ceramic enamels in different colours
Small paintbrush
Clear polyurethane varnish

1 Wash the china pot in warm soapy water to remove any grease or grime. Allow to dry thoroughly.

Choose a colour scheme and apply the first shade of paint carefully using a small paintbrush.

2 Paint in the areas chosen for the second colour, wiping off any paint that might go over the edge of a particular detail.

3 Continue to paint in the design until the china pot is decorated all over.

Allow the paint to dry thoroughly. For extra protection apply a coat of clear varnish.

DESIGN IN THE NEGATIVE

Draw on a white plate with a black chinagraph pencil and then colour the remaining areas. The chinagraph pencil marks are then rubbed away, leaving white lines in their place. Make sure the ceramic enamels are of the non-toxic variety.

YOU WILL NEED
Black chinagraph pencil
White china plate
Ceramic enamels
Small paintbrush
Paper towel or tissue paper

1 Using the chinagraph pencil, draw your design onto the plate.

2 Paint in the larger areas of colour. If you wish to mix colours, make sure you mix enough. Ceramic enamels look better slightly dappled, as it is very difficult to achieve a flat even surface over a large area.

3 When the large areas have been painted, fill in the details. Do not overload the brush with paint but build up the colour gradually. Leave the paint to dry. Rub away the chinagraph pencil marks using a paper towel or tissue paper.

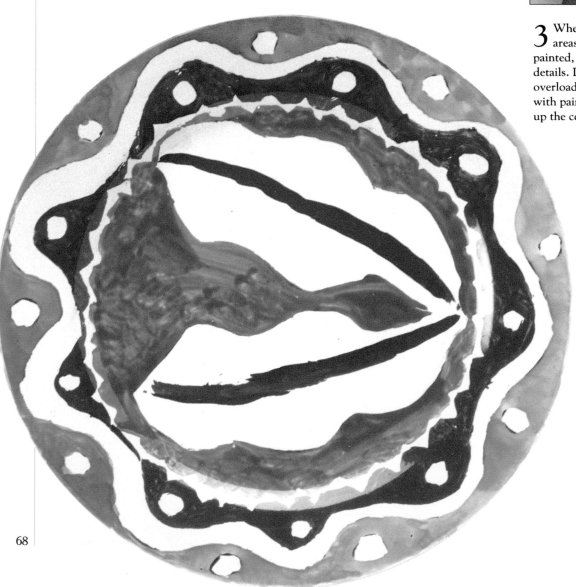

EGGCUPS

These eggcups will help to get your day off to a good start! They are bright and jazzy, and take their inspiration from European folk art designs. As when painting all crockery, make absolutely sure that you are using non-toxic cold ceramic enamels, and do *not* paint any surface that comes directly into contact with food. Bon appetit!

YOU WILL NEED
600 ml (1 pt) warm water with 10 ml (2 tsp) vinegar
Chinagraph pencil
Plain white eggcups
Cold ceramic enamels in a variety of colours
Paintbrushes in various sizes

1 Wash each eggcup in the vinegar solution to remove any grease. Dry thoroughly. Draw your design directly onto the china using a chinagraph pencil.

2 Start to fill in the first colour of enamel. Work from the lightest shades to the darkest, so that you can paint on top of initial coats of enamel if you like.

3 Continue to paint in the design.

4 For a bolder effect, first block in the design with bright colours, and then outline with black enamel.

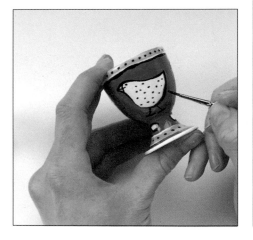

PLANT POT

A fern or other non-flowering house plant looks very effective in this plain white pot with a bold stencilled design.

YOU WILL NEED

15 cm (6 in) white china plant pot
4 cm (1½ in) wide masking tape
Pencil
Craft knife
Ceramic enamels in 2 basic colours
Small plate for paints
2 small pieces of sponge
Plastic glove

1 Cover the rim of the pot with masking tape, overlapping the outer edge by 12 mm (½ in). Cover the side of the pot with masking tape, leaving a 4 cm (1½ in) space between each strip of tape. Draw a flower design on each strip of tape and pencil in the parts to be cut out.

2 Holding the pot firmly with one hand, take the craft knife with the other and carefully cut out the shapes drawn onto the masking tape. Peel off the cut-out tape as you go along. Continue until the design is complete all round the pot.

3 Pour a little paint onto a plate. Using a small piece of sponge, dab the first colour onto alternating cut-out spaces. Repeat with the second colour. Wear a plastic glove on the hand you use to apply the paint to protect yourself from splashes. Sponge under the rim and around the base of the pot. Leave to dry thoroughly. When dry, peel off all the masking tape.

STENCILLED TRINKET BOX

This charming trinket box can be used to keep many things such as coins, keys or spare buttons. The traditional method of stencilling enables you to repeat a design quickly and easily.

YOU WILL NEED

Round box
White matt emulsion paint
Small paintbrush
Pencil
Plain paper
Tape measure
Clear acetate
Black felt-tip pen
Craft knife
Masking tape
Blue acrylic paint
Stipple brush
Clear polyurethane varnish

2 Lift the stencil carefully and tape it down onto the lid. Stipple it with undiluted blue acrylic paint, using a dry stipple brush. Leave to dry.

3 Repeat this process for the side design, remembering to tape down the stencil, moving it around the box as necessary.

1 Prime the box with a coat of white matt emulsion paint. Draw around the lid onto a sheet of plain paper to get the correct size for the design. Measure the circumference and depth of the box and transfer these measurements onto the paper. Scale up the design within the measurements. Place the box lid on the acetate, draw around it with a felt-tip pen and then cut out the shape. Stick down the acetate onto the lid design with masking tape. Cut out the stencil with a craft knife. Repeat this process to make the stencil for the side design.

4 Paint the rim of the lid with blue acrylic paint. Leave to dry and then coat with clear polyurethane varnish to protect the box.

Choose a pattern that will look good repeated on the head of the notelets. If you have not used stencils previously, it is best to practise on newspaper before working on expensive writing paper.

YOU WILL NEED
Sheets of coloured writing paper
Strip of stiff card
Pencil
Scissors
Assorted poster paints
Small plate
Small round stencil brush or small sponge
Soft cloth

1 Fold the sheets of writing paper in half. Take the strip of card and concertina into 15 mm (⅝ in) folds.

2 Keep the card folded and draw out a pattern. Cut out using scissors. Open the pattern out flat and lay it across the top of the folded writing paper.

3 Mix a little poster paint on a small plate. Dab the stencil brush or sponge into the paint, wiping off any surplus on a soft cloth. It is very important not to overload the brush or sponge with paint if you want to avoid smudges.

Place the cut-out card onto the head of the folded sheet of writing paper, holding the card firmly in position with one hand. Dab paint through the opening of the cut-outs. Lift up the card gently and leave the paper to dry.

ROSE CARD

This romantic birthday card is very effective, particularly on the black background colour which adds depth to the stencilled single rose.

YOU WILL NEED

Square of stiff card
Ruler
Pencil
Plain paper
Masking tape
Clear acetate twice the size of the folded card
Craft knife
Natural sponge
Assorted acrylic paints
Small paintbrush

1 Fold the square of stiff card in half, scoring along the inside line. Measure the front of the card to ensure your design fits the available space. Draw a rose design onto plain paper, taping it down onto a clean flat board. Cover the design with half of the acetate and tape down. Cut out only the shape of the rose. Remove the stencil carefully. Move the acetate up so that the bottom half covers the design. Repeat the cutting process, only this time cut out only the shape of the leaves.

2 Place the stencil of the leaves onto the card, securing with the masking tape and making sure the stencil is central. Moisten the natural sponge, squeezing out any excess water. Use green and white acrylic paint for the leaves, making sure the paint is not too wet. Fade the sponging from the edge towards the middle of the leaves. Leave to dry and remove carefully.

3 Place the stencil of the rose carefully onto the centre of the card, moving it around until it fits snugly in the middle of the bed of leaves. Repeat the process with pink and white acrylic paint, again fading the stippling with the natural sponge in towards the middle. Leave to dry and remove the acetate carefully.

4 Add a finishing touch with a twirl of paint using a paintbrush, and your card is completed.

COSMIC STATIONERY

The intricate design of shooting stars and fireworks demands neat fingers and plenty of patience! Use the stencil to make a harlequin set of writing paper in a variety of colours.

YOU WILL NEED

Strip of stiff card
Masking tape
Pencil
Craft knife
Sheets of coloured writing paper
Poster paint in assorted colours
Round stencil brush or small sponge
Soft cloth

1 Cover a strip of stiff card completely with strips of masking tape. Using a pencil draw a design of shooting stars and fireworks on it. Working on a hard-surfaced board and using a craft knife cut out all the shapes carefully to form the stencil template.

2 Place the stencil over a sheet of writing paper, and secure in position with a little masking tape. Have your paints ready on a plate. Dab the brush or sponge into each colour, wiping off any surplus on a soft cloth. It is very important not to overload the brush or sponge with paint if you want to avoid smudges. Dab the paints through the stencil until the design is completed. Lift up the stencil gently and leave the paper to dry.

STENCILLED TRAY

The traditional technique of stencilling is an extremely effective form of decoration. This tray is pretty enough to be displayed in your kitchen when not in use. Why not try using colours to match a favourite set of china?

YOU WILL NEED
Wooden tray
White matt emulsion paint
Large paintbrush
Sandpaper
Masking tape
Diluted blue acrylic paint
Stipple brush
Sheet of plain paper
Pencil
Clear acetate
Craft knife
Clear satin polyurethane varnish

1 Prepare the tray. Prime with white matt emulsion paint, rub down with sandpaper and give it another coat for a nice smooth finish. When the paint is dry, put masking tape all along the inside edges of the tray. Brush diluted blue acrylic paint thinly onto the edges of the tray and stipple off while the paint is still wet; work swiftly and only do a section at a time so that the paint does not have a chance to dry.

2 Draw your design onto plain paper, stick the paper down onto a smooth board and then place a sheet of acetate on top, making sure you stick it down on top of the design with masking tape. Place on a hard surface and start to cut out the shapes of your stencil very carefully, using a craft knife and holding down the acetate with your free hand where necessary.

3 When you have finished cutting out the design, transfer the stencil onto the tray, remembering to remove the masking tape very carefully. Tape down the stencil in the centre of the tray. It is also a good idea to tape down some paper around the edges of the acetate so that splashes of blue do not go on to the surrounding area. Stipple on the paint with a dry stipple brush using fairly dry acrylic paint; get rid of any excess paint before beginning by stippling on a scrap of paper. Leave to dry, remove the stencil and give the tray two coats of clear satin polyurethane varnish.

PHOTO FRAME

Jazz up a favourite photograph with a simple stencilled frame. Choose colours that enhance those in the photograph and mount it on the wall for all to see. If a stencil is made for one frame, it can be used again to make a series.

YOU WILL NEED
Thick coloured card
Metal rule
Craft knife
Thin card
Clear acetate
Permanent black ink pen
Masking tape
Stencil brush
Acrylic paint
Clear glue
Picture hanger

1 First draw up the pieces of your frame on thick coloured card. Then carefully cut these out using a metal rule and craft knife. In the same way, cut three spacers out of thin card.

2 Take a piece of clear acetate of the same width as the front frame piece and draw on the design with a permanent black ink pen. Then cut out the design with a sharp craft knife.

3 Place the acetate on the front frame piece, securing it with masking tape. Using a stencil brush with a little acrylic paint, stipple on the paint. Allow the paint to dry before removing the acetate.

4 Glue the three spacers onto the sides and the bottom to the back of the stencilled frame piece. Then stick the spacers to the back piece of coloured card frame.

5 When the frame is complete, attach a light picture hanger to the back, strengthen with masking tape, and hang on the wall.

STAR SCARF

Stencilling a plain scarf is a wonderful way to show off your artistic talent and look original.

YOU WILL NEED
Thin card
Clear acetate
Permanent black ink pen
Craft knife
Scarf
Masking tape
Fabric paints
Stencil brush
Iron
Tissue paper

1 Make a star template in thin card to fit the scarf. Draw round the template onto clear acetate using a permanent black ink pen. Cut out the star image from the clear acetate, following the black lines using a craft knife.

2 Secure the acetate stencil on a corner of the scarf with masking tape. Put a little fabric paint onto the stencil brush and stipple the paint straight onto the fabric. Start at the tip of each star point and lightly work towards the middle. Concentrate more on the points and edges to get a 3-dimensional look.

3 Repeat on all four corners and the centre of the scarf and allow to dry. Iron the star images with a medium hot iron. Place a piece of tissue paper between the iron and the fabric to protect the paint. The heat of the iron fixes the fabric paint so that it can be washed.

SEAHORSE SHIRT

Transform a white cotton turtle-neck with a stencilled design of an exotic seahorse painted in three bright colours.

YOU WILL NEED
Thin card
Craft knife
Black felt-tip pen
Thick card cut to turtle-neck size
White cotton turtle-neck
Masking tape
3 round stencil brushes
Fabric paints in 3 colours
Small plate
Fine flat brush

1 Cut a piece of thin card to fit the area of the front of the turtle-neck you would like to decorate. Scale up the design to the required size. Insert the thick card inside the shirt to stretch the fabric, and prevent the paint from leaking onto the back.

2 Place the design on a hard-surfaced board and cut out all the black shapes carefully. This is your stencil.

3 Secure the stencil on the front of the turtle-neck using masking tape. Hold the stencil brush vertically and dab the paint through the cut-out holes of the stencil. Change colours and brushes as you go along. When you have finished colouring the design lift up the stencil carefully and put it aside to dry. If there are any smudges, touch up carefully with a fine flat brush. Leave the turtle-neck to dry thoroughly. Remove the piece of thick card. Fix according to the instructions on the paints.

FLOWER POT STENCIL

Enhance your plant with an individual flower pot. Decorate a terracotta plant pot to give it individuality; try varying the sizes for a whole collection.

YOU WILL NEED
Terracotta flower pot
Clear acetate
Permanent black ink pen
Craft knife
Masking tape
Acrylic paint
Small stencil brush

1 Wash the flower pot thoroughly with soapy water so that all grease and dirt marks are removed. Leave to dry thoroughly. Scale up the flower design from the template. Then draw it onto clear acetate with a permanent black ink pen. Cut around the black pen lines on the acetate carefully using a sharp craft knife.

2 Secure the acetate stencil onto the terracotta flower pot with masking tape. Then apply the acrylic paint directly onto the terracotta pot through the acetate, using a stencil brush. Use small amounts of paint; if too much is applied, it may leak under the acetate. Do not remove the acetate until the paint is dry.

3 Move the acetate stencil around the pot repeating the process until you are satisfied with the total design.

Clear acetate has the advantage of your being able to see through it for perfect placement when spacing your design.

CAT CUSHION

Most 'bean bag' cushions are very popular with pets, but this one with its additional filling of catmint (irresistible to cats) with tansy and cotton lavender (which fleas and other fur 'visitors' hate) should make for a very happy cat.

YOU WILL NEED

Lengths of cotton and calico (muslin) fabrics
Scissors
Needle and thread
½ cupful of dried tansy
½ cupful of dried catmint (nepeta)
½ cupful of dried cotton lavender (santolina)
1 heaped teaspoon of orrisroot powder
Small polystyrene (styrofoam) 'pearls' for filling

1 Cut out two pieces each of the calico (muslin) and your chosen cotton outer cover fabric, measuring 50 cm × 41 cm (19½ in × 16 in). Stitch the two short sides and one long side of the calico together, and part of the remaining long side, leaving a 7.5 cm (3 in) opening. Turn through. Repeat with the cover fabric, remembering to start with the material inside out. Leave a bigger opening so that the filled calico inner can be inserted.

2 Mix the tansy, catmint, cotton lavender and orrisroot powder together in a bowl. Make up a calico sachet about 10 cm (4 in) square, fill with the special cat pot-pourri and sew together. Fill the calico inner with the polystyrene 'pearls', pop in the sachet and sew together.

3 Slide the calico-covered cushion into the outer cover and slipstitch the gap.

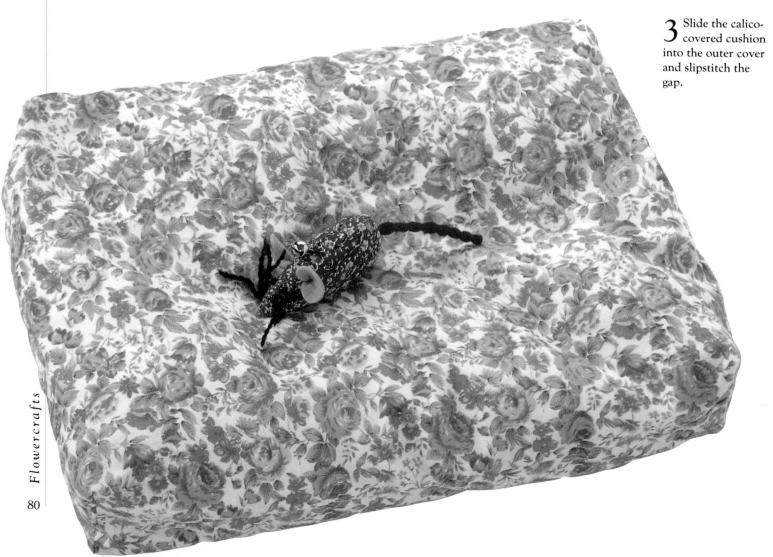

POT-POURRI

This simple and lightly spiced pot-pourri has a careful selection of material, chosen for its appearance in a basket as well as for its perfume.

YOU WILL NEED

3 cupfuls dried blue larkspur flowers, a few dried red roses for colour, 1 cupful geranium leaves, 1 cupful of soapwort leaves and flowers

1 teaspoon grated lemon rind

½ teaspoon sandalwood powder for smell

½ cupful orrisroot powder (perfume fixative)

Mixing bowl

5 drops of geranium essential oil for smell

Plastic ice-cream container with tight-fitting lid

Sticky tape

Display bowl or basket

Lace ribbon

1 Remove the larkspur florets from the stems and break up the roses, reserving some whole for decoration.

2 Add the geranium leaves, soapwort leaves and flowers, lemon rind, sandalwood and orrisroot powders.

Place all the ingredients in a mixing bowl and stir gently as you slowly drip in the geranium essential oil.

3 Transfer the mixture to a plastic ice-cream container and seal the lid carefully with sticky tape. Store in a warm place for 6 weeks, stirring occasionally. When the pot-pourri is ready, empty into a display bowl, or fill a small basket. Decorate with a small bunch of larkspur and roses tied with a lace ribbon.

TABLE DECORATION

This soft, delicate arrangement is an ideal table decoration for a small or intimate dinner party and a chance to display that very special plate.

YOU WILL NEED
Florist's adhesive clay tape
Florist's scissors
Plastic pin holders
Small pretty plate
Florist's plasticine (putty)
2 plastic candle holders
Scrim ribbon
Silver and black reel wires
Florist's wire cutters
Reindeer moss
Dried larkspur
Fir cones
Dried roses
Candles

1 Cut a short length of florist's adhesive clay tape and use it to fix a florist's plastic pin holder off-centre on your chosen pretty plate.

2 Knead a piece of florist's plasticine (putty) into a 5 cm (2 in) diameter ball and fix onto the pin holder. Push two plastic candle holders into this.

3 Cut several 15 cm (6 in) lengths of scrim ribbon and form into single loops using silver reel wire.

4 Cut 5 cm (2 in) pieces of silver reel wire and bend into hairpin shapes. Cover the candle holders and clay with pieces of reindeer moss, securing it in place with the wire pins.

5 Wire the larkspur and fir cones using black reel wire.

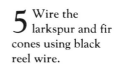

6 Cut down rose stems to suitable lengths. Start to place the various elements, by pushing into the florist's plasticine (putty). Insert the ribbon loops to simulate bows and disguise the candle holders. Finally place the two candles in their holders. Take great care not to let lighted candles burn down near the decorations.

SCENTED NOTEPAPER

The tradition of 'scenting' notepaper goes back many centuries; often a drop of the sender's favourite scent was used but this stained the paper. It is much better to leave a lavender sachet with the paper for a month.

YOU WILL NEED

Muslin (cheesecloth)
Needle and thread
½ cupful lavender flowers
Handmade or fine acid-free notepaper
Pressed flowers
Tweezers
Rubber-based adhesive
Toothpick
Box or bag
Sticky tape
Cellophane

1 Make up a square sachet of muslin and fill with lavender.

2 Decorate the notepaper using pressed flowers. Arrange the flowers or petals using tweezers, sticking them in place with a dab of rubber-based adhesive applied with a toothpick.

3 Put the notepaper in a box – or a bag if you do not have a box big enough – with the sachet and seal the box. Leave for a month. Take the notepaper out of the box or bag, and wrap it in cellophane to keep in the perfume.

PRESSED FLOWER CANDLE

Making these candles is challenging, but good fun. Turn a plain white candle into an elegant decorated gift that will give hours of pleasure.

YOU WILL NEED
Heatproof cylindrical container (taller and wider than the candle)
4-5 cm (1½-2 in) diameter white candle
Selection of pressed flowers, leaves or grasses

1 Fill the container with enough hot water to reach the shoulder of the candle when it is immersed. Holding the candle by the wick, immerse in the hot water for about 30 seconds. Remove the candle, and working quickly, press a few leaves and flowers onto the softened wax around the lower part of the candle.

2 Refill the container with very hot water and dip the candle again briefly to soften the wax surface and seal in the pressed flowers.

ROSEBUD POMANDER

This long-lasting pomander looks beautiful and its perfume can be renewed when necessary with a few drops of rose essential oil.

YOU WILL NEED

90 cm × 12 mm (36 in × ½ in) green
    satin ribbon
Length of florist's wire
9 cm (3½ in) diameter florist's foam
    (styrofoam) ball
Dried rosebuds of different sizes
White woodworking glue or rubber-
    based glue
Paste brush
Rose essential oil

1 Cut the ribbon into 3 equal lengths. Tie a bow in the centre of each piece of ribbon leaving two long ends. Tie the third piece into a double bow and leave the ends long to make a hanging loop. Twist a florist's wire around each bow leaving one long end and push the wires through the foam ball. Pull the bows down to the ball and tuck in the end of each wire to secure.

2 Grade the rosebuds from smallest to largest. Divide the ball into quarters by painting a line of glue and pressing in a row of medium-sized rosebuds along it.

3 Cover one quarter at a time with glue and press in rosebuds, the smallest at the top and bottom and getting larger as you reach the centre, until the ball is completely covered. A few drops of rose essential oil can now be dripped onto the pomander ball.

PRESSED FLOWER CARD

Winter months are the time to use the flowers that you pressed in the summer. It is fun arranging them into a picture, which makes such a lasting gift when covered with protective film, available from specialist suppliers. Folded cards are available from most artist's suppliers.

YOU WILL NEED
Rubber-based adhesive
Small dish
Selection of dried flowers including verbena, forget-me-not, spiraea and gypsophila (baby's breath) and foliage
Folded blank card with aperture
Tweezers
Toothpick
Heat-sealing protective covering film
Steam iron

1 Squeeze out a little adhesive onto a small dish. Start by positioning foliage in an irregular oval shape to fit within the cut-out aperture of the card. Fix the foliage in position using tweezers to pick up each leaf. Using a toothpick transfer the smallest spot of adhesive to the reverse side of the leaf and touch it down.

2 Position and touch down verbena and forget- me-not flowers in the same way.

3 Use florets of spiraea and gypsophilia (baby's breath) to complete your design.

4 Protect the design with iron-on heat sealing laminate. Cut out a piece of the laminate slightly smaller than the page size. Open up the card and cover the design with the sheet of protective film, and iron down in accordance with the manufacturer's instructions. Re-fold the completed card.

FESTIVE
WREATH

The materials and colours for this wreath have been chosen to suit any festival or occasion from an anniversary or birthday to Christmas. All the items are readily available from craft or florist's suppliers. A spring or summer wreath can be made using the flowers available.

YOU WILL NEED
Florist's scissors
Dried nigella orientalis seed-heads
Florist's foam (styrofoam) wreath base
Florist's wire cutters
Bunches of artificial fruit and leaves
Dried ambrociana
Florist's black and silver reel wires
Lace ribbons
Dried red roses

1 Cut short stems of nigella orientalis, and insert around the inner circumference of a foam wreath at an angle of about 15°.

2 Cut down the wires of the bunches of artificial fruit and leaves to about 4 cm (1½ in) in length, and insert around the top of the wreath at regular intervals.

3 Wire together small bunches of ambrociana with florist's black reel

wire and insert all around the outside of the wreath to form a soft edge.

4 Cut eight 30 cm (12 in) lengths of ribbon to make bows with two loops and two ends. Bind with florist's silver reel wire, leaving two ends, and insert evenly

around the wreath. Then cut five 12.5 cm (5 in) lengths. Fold in half, bind with florist's silver reel wire at the centre and insert around the outer edge of the wreath.

5 Position the roses evenly around the centre of the wreath and fill in with more

nigella and ambrociana where required to give a balanced effect.

LAVENDER BAG

These lavender bags, smelling so fresh and clean, make very pretty gifts that look charming and are so practical in a linen cupboard.

YOU WILL NEED

35 cm × 6 mm (14 in × ¼ in) ribbon
28 cm × 5 cm (11 in × 2 in) piece of
    lace
Scissors
4 pieces of muslin (cheesecloth), each
    12.5 cm × 10 cm (5 in × 4 in)
Needle and thread
Lavender pot-pourri
5 stems of lavender
Small elastic band

1 Cut a 12.5 cm (5 in) length of ribbon and lace. Place a length of lace and one of ribbon 7.5 cm (3 in) from the bottom edge of a piece of muslin (cheese-cloth) and stitch into place. Gather the remaining length of lace and stitch to the top of the muslin.

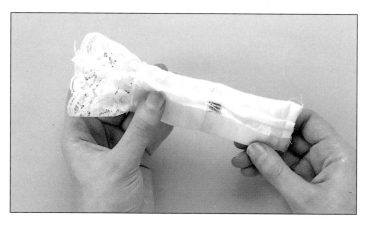

2 Turn through and stitch the sides. Fold to the centre seam, stitch the bottom edge and turn through.

3 Fill with the lavender pot-pourri and tuck the five stems of lavender into the top of the bag, protruding from the neck, and secure with an elastic band.

4 Take the remaining ribbon and tie in a bow around the neck, to cover the elastic band.

FLOWER POSY

The posy is a very old form of flower arrangement with its origins dating from the medieval nosegay. Using dried and silk flowers means it can be treasured as a keepsake for years to come.

YOU WILL NEED

Florist's foam (styrofoam) posy holder and ready-formed lace frill
Dried gypsophila (baby's breath)
Florist's scissors
Florist's silver reel wire
Florist's wire cutters
Stems of silk peony flowers, buds and leaves
Sticky tape
2.5 cm (1 in) wide length of cream silk ribbon

1 Fix the frill around the foam head of the holder by pulling it down until it is firmly in place.

2 Cut short heads of gypsophila and wire together with silver reel wire.

3 Remove the leaves from the peony stems and insert a row around the edge of the foam block.

4 Cut the stem of a peony bud and insert into the centre of the foam block, and position open flowers around the edge.

5 Add more leaves and peonies. Fill in by inserting bunches of wired gypsophila to create an even but soft effect.

6 Tape the ribbon to the end of the handle and bind upwards towards the under-side of the posy. Secure with sticky tape. Make several 'figures of eight' from the remaining ribbon and bind at the centre to form a multiple bow. Wire to the base of the posy to cover the back. Stick down.

HERBAL BATH SACHETS

These scented sachets hang under the hot water when the bath tub is being filled. They create a refreshing fragrance as well as being naturally soothing and softening for the skin.

YOU WILL NEED

1 cupful oatmeal
½ cupful powdered milk
¼ cupful wheat bran
Handful of dried lavender or
 rosemary flowers
Handful of soapwort leaves and
 flowers
Plastic bowl
Teaspoon
Nappy (diaper) liners or thin
 cheesecloth
6mm (¼ in) wide ribbon or string
Pinking shears

1 Mix all the ingredients together in a plastic bowl.

2 Place two teaspoons of the mixture in the centre of a nappy (diaper) liner. Gather up the liner around the mixture and tie with a ribbon or string, leaving ends long enough for the sachet to hang beneath the running water.

3 Cut off the corners of the nappy liners using pinking shears and arrange so that you achieve a pretty frill.

SCENTED SHELLS

As sea shells are generally associated with water, the ideal place to display a collection is in the bathroom. Add a further pleasing dimension to their colour and form by making them fragrant.

YOU WILL NEED
Collection of sea shells
Dish-washing liquid
Bleach
Towel
1 vanilla pod (bean)
Small cuttlefish bone
Lemon, bay and rosemary essential oils
Plastic ice-cream container with tight-fitting lid
Glass dish or bowl

1 Scrub and wash the shells carefully in soapy water to which a little bleach has been added, and set aside to dry thoroughly on a towel.

2 Moisten a cuttlefish bone with 25 drops of lemon, 15 drops of bay and 5 drops of rosemary essential oils. Place a bruised vanilla pod and the cuttlefish bone into a plastic ice-cream container. Add the shells, seal down the lid and leave for 4 weeks. Remove half the shells and arrange in a glass dish or bowl for display. After a few weeks or whenever the shells lose their fragrance, replace with the other shells left in the container. Do this on a regular basis, and occasionally refresh the cuttlefish bone with a few drops of the essential oils.

ALMOND BUBBLE BATH

This bubble bath makes a delightful gift – it is excellent for the skin, adds a beautiful perfume and foams when a little is poured slowly under fast-running hot water, when you are starting to fill the bathtub. It also looks good displayed in the bathroom.

YOU WILL NEED
300 ml (½ pint) non-biological
  dishwashing liquid
Screw-top jar
15 drops peach essential oil
2 drops pink food colouring
2 tablespoons almond oil
Presentation bottle
Label

1 Pour the dishwashing liquid into the screw-top jar and add the peach essential oil and food colouring.

2 Add the almond oil, screw on the lid and shake vigorously for about a minute. Fill the presentation bottle immediately. Decorate the bottle as liked and label carefully with a list of the contents and instructions to shake the bottle for a few seconds before use.

SUGGESTED LABEL:

> ### ALMOND BUBBLE BATH
> A mild soap base combines with peach essential oil to produce foaming frothy pink bubbles for a gentle soak in the bath tub.

SWEET VIOLET CREAM

This sweet-smelling rich beauty cream makes an interesting change to the usual commercially produced cosmetics.

YOU WILL NEED

1 teaspoon beeswax
3 tablespoons almond oil
Heatproof mixing bowl
Small saucepan
Newspaper
½ teaspoon cornflour (cornstarch)
2 tablespoons boiling water
Balloon or electric whisk
6 drops violet essential oil
Presentation jar
Label

1 Melt the beeswax in the almond oil in a bowl over a saucepan of hot water. When melted, remove the bowl and stand on some folded newspaper.

2 Add the cornflour (cornstarch), stir well and then add the water gradually, beating with the whisk until the mixture becomes creamy.

3 Add the violet essential oil, and continue to whisk until the cream is cool. Then pour into the presentation jar and leave to set. Label with a list of the contents.

SPICE AND LEMON COLOGNE

This cologne with its fresh, spicy aroma makes a super gift for any man. The miniature bottles are ideal for packing when travelling.

YOU WILL NEED

2 handfuls of lemon geranium leaves
Sharp knife
2 cinnamon sticks
Screw-top jar for mixing
3 teaspoons grated lemon rind
1½ cups vodka (or ethyl alcohol)
Coffee filter paper
Plastic or glass funnel
Small glass jug
Presentation miniature bottles
Labels

1 Wash the geranium leaves, pat dry and chop finely. Break up the cinnamon sticks and pack with the leaves into the jar. Add the grated lemon rind to the jar and fill with vodka. Secure the lid and store in a warm place for 4 weeks, shaking daily.

2 Filter the mixture through a coffee filter paper in a funnel into a jug. Repeat if the liquid is not very clear.

Wash and dry the storage jar and pour in the filtered cologne. Put the lid on the jar and keep in a dark place for 6 months.

3 Taking care not to disturb any sediment, decant the liquid carefully into the miniature bottles and label with the contents.

ROSE MOISTURIZER

This moisturizer, made from natural ingredients, is light, nourishing and soothing and will make a most welcome gift.

YOU WILL NEED

1 teaspoon beeswax
3 teaspoons lanolin
Small heatproof mixing bowl
Small non-aluminium saucepan
3 tablespoons almond oil
150 ml (¼ pint) rose-water
Pinch of borax
Cooking thermometer
Balloon whisk
Screw-top presentation jar
Label

1 Melt the beeswax and lanolin in a small mixing bowl resting in the saucepan of hot water over a low heat. Add the almond oil and beat together. Put the mixing bowl in a warm place.

2 Wash and dry the saucepan. Heat the rose-water and borax to about 50°C (122°F) and add slowly to the mixing bowl. Whisk the mixture together.

3 Stand the bowl in cold water and continue whisking until the cream is cold. The cream will still be soft and can be spooned into the presentation jar. Label with a list of contents.

AROMATIC BODY OIL

Almond oil can be bought inexpensively in large quantities from specialist shops. It is very light and soothing to the skin and is specially beneficial with this exotic blend of essential oils. Remember that essential oils are very strong, and should never be used undiluted directly on the skin. If some is splashed on by accident, wash it off immediately with soap and water. The body oil can be used after baths, or rubbed on elbows, knees and hands at any time.

1 Pour the almond oil into the screw-top jar.

YOU WILL NEED
150 ml (¼ pint) almond oil
Screw-top jar for mixing
15 drops peach essential oil
10 drops melissa essential oil
Presentation bottles
Labels

2 Add the peach and melissa essential oils, drop by drop. Secure the lid and shake for 1 minute. Leave for 1 hour before pouring into the presentation bottles. Label with contents.

SUGGESTED LABEL:

> ### AROMATIC BODY OIL
> A refreshing and soothing body oil for use after bathing or on dry skin at any time, with the delicate scents of peach and melissa essential oils.

PEPPERMINT FOOT-BATH

This rejuvenating pick-me-up for tired and aching feet would be much appreciated by a busy hostess hard at work. The given quantity will be enough for four foot-baths. To use, fill a large bowl with moderately hot water, stir in the peppermint mixture and soak the feet for 10 minutes.

YOU WILL NEED
Several stems of fresh peppermint or
    60 g (2 oz) dried peppermint leaves
125 g (4 oz) juniper berries
Non-aluminium saucepan with lid
750 ml (1¼ pints) water
12 drops sandalwood essential oil
6 drops cypress essential oil
Coffee filter paper
Funnel
Storage jars or bottles
Labels

1 Place the peppermint and juniper in the saucepan, add the water and heat slowly to just below boiling point, stirring occasionally. Cover the saucepan and leave to cool.

2 Before the mixture is cold, add the sandalwood and cypress essential oils and stir well.

3 Strain off the liquid through a coffee filter paper in a funnel into the storage jars. Seal and label with instructions on how to use and a list of contents.

ROSEMARY HAIR RINSE

This rosemary rinse should be massaged into the scalp as a final rinse to make the hair beautifully soft and well-conditioned.

YOU WILL NEED
2 handfuls of fresh rosemary stems
2 jars with plastic screw-tops
600 ml (1 pint) white vinegar
600 ml (1 pint) water
Non-aluminium saucepan
Coffee filter paper
Funnel
Presentation bottles
Labels

1 Wash the rosemary stems carefully in cold water and shake dry. Break into manageable lengths and divide between the jars.

2 Put the vinegar and water in a saucepan and bring to the boil. Leave to stand for 2 minutes and pour over the rosemary in the jars. Stand on a warm window-sill for 2 weeks, shaking occasionally. Then strain the liquid through a coffee filter paper in a funnel into the presentation bottles. Label with a list of the contents and instructions on how to use.

SCENTED BATH SALTS

This is a very easy way to make beautifully scented, coloured bath salts. You can use any colouring and any variety of essential oil you like.

YOU WILL NEED

3 tablespoons vodka
Small yogurt pot
Pink food colouring
Peach essential oil
1 teaspoon almond oil
Plastic spoon
1 kg (2 lb) washing soda crystals
1 litre (1¾ pint) plastic ice-cream
    container with a well-fitting lid
Presentation jars
Ribbon
Labels

1 Pour the vodka into the clean yogurt pot, and add about 5 drops of pink food colouring, 15 drops of peach essential oil and the almond oil. Stir until the mixture is thoroughly blended.

2 Put the washing soda crystals into the ice-cream container, give the vodka mixture a final stir, and pour it over carefully. Keep turning the crystals over with a plastic spoon for a few minutes, and then seal with the lid.

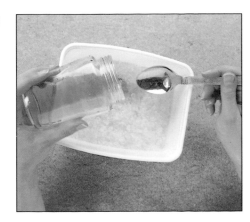

3 After 3 days, stir the bath salts again and pack into attractive jars. Add a ribbon bow and label with the contents.

MARINATED OLIVES

A jar of these marinated olives makes an original hostess gift. As they will cause a minor explosion on the palate, warn people when offering them at a drinks party with other nibbles!

YOU WILL NEED

Jar of pitted black olives in brine
Jar of pitted green olives in brine
Sieve
1 fresh hot chilli
3 cloves of garlic
Chopping board and knife
Storage jar
5 ml (1 tsp) dried oregano
Olive oil
Presentation jar
Label

1 Empty the jars of olives into a sieve and rinse thoroughly under a running cold tap. Set aside to drain. Chop the chilli and garlic very finely and put into the storage jar with the oregano. Add a little oil and shake well.

2 Add the drained olives and enough oil to cover. Shake gently for a minute every day for a week, then transfer to the presentation jar, topping up with more olive oil if necessary. Label the jar, listing all the ingredients.

ALMOND TREATS

While these 'fruits' are traditionally eaten at Christmas, they also make a super gift at any time of the year. Try to use white marzipan (almond paste) which will enable you to mix more realistic colours.

YOU WILL NEED
White marzipan (almond paste)
Sharp knife
Board
Rolling pin
Gel food colourings
Icing (confectioners') sugar
Toothpicks
Petits fours paper cases
Lidded container
Greaseproof (wax) paper

1 Divide the marzipan (almond paste) into pieces for the basic colouring. Roll out one piece thinly. Dot the food colouring very lightly on the surface. Then knead the marzipan (almond paste) until it is evenly coloured. Repeat this process for each colour.

2 Mould the marzipan (almond paste) into appropriate fruit shapes to suit the different colours. Use a little extra colouring in some areas.

3 Use icing (confectioners') sugar to achieve a soft or peach-like effect, and food colourings on the tip of a toothpick to define areas, add 'blemishes' and colour stems. Place the fruit in petits fours cases to protect them and enhance their appearance. Store in a lidded container, lined with grease-proof paper, until they are packed into a presentation box.

HERB BUTTER

Decorative containers filled with herb-flavoured butters make thoughtful gifts for busy cooks. Rosemary butter is good with green peas and roast lamb, mint with new potatoes, and fennel with fish.

YOU WILL NEED
Fresh herbs of your choice
Paper towels
Chopping board
Sharp knife or herb chopper
Best quality unsalted butter
Salt
Saucers or small mixing bowls
Spatula

2 Cut up the unsalted butter into medium-sized pieces and allow to soften at room temperature.

Sprinkle a little salt over the herbs — this will help to crush the herbs and release their flavour.

1 Rinse small bunches of herbs carefully in cold water and pat dry with paper towels. Chop each herb very finely on a chopping board, keeping each herb separate.

3 Mix the herbs with the softened butter using a spatula. When thoroughly mixed together pack into decorative containers and chill in the refrigerator until required.

GINGERBREAD TREES

Try baking a light gingerbread mixture in decorative Christmas tree shapes, and edge with icing (confectioners') sugar 'snow'. Finish them off with pretty seasonal ribbon bows.

YOU WILL NEED
100 g (4 oz/1 stick) butter, slightly softened
100 g (4 oz/⅔ cup) soft brown sugar
100 g (4 oz/½ cup) golden (corn) syrup
2 eggs
Sieve
450 g (1 lb/4 cups) white self-raising flour
15 ml (1 tbsp) ground ginger
Rolling pin and board
Christmas-tree shape cutter
Baking sheet
Ribbon
Shallow dish
Icing (confectioners') sugar

1 Beat the butter, sugar and golden (corn) syrup into a cream and then beat in the eggs. Sift in the flour and ground ginger and mix into a dough.

2 Roll the dough out thinly and stamp out Christmas tree shapes. Arrange on an oiled baking sheet. Bake for 20 minutes at 180°C (350°F/gas 4).

3 When cool, tie a ribbon bow on each tree shape and then dip the sides carefully in a shallow dish containing about 6 mm (¼ in) depth of icing (confectioners') sugar to decorate the upper edges of the branches with 'snow'.

ROSE AND JASMINE TEAS

Both rose and jasmine teas are lightly but beautifully flavoured, are drunk without milk, and are delicious either hot or cold. Dried rose and jasmine petals are available from specialist suppliers. Green 'gunpowder' teas are made with large leaves which, like the petals, will sink, so they are suitable for using when making tea directly in a cup or glass. Only use half a teaspoon for each cup.

YOU WILL NEED

Rose petals
Net bag
Lemon zest-peeler or sharp knife
Lemon
Plate
Dried jasmine petals
Gunpowder tea
Airtight storage containers

1 To dry your own rose petals, choose a variety that is sweet rather than bitter-tasting. Half-fill a little net bag with rose petals and hang in a warm dark place until dry.

2 Using a lemon zest-peeler or a sharp knife, remove only the zest (no pith) from a lemon, shred finely and leave to dry on a plate in the bottom of a cooling oven for 30 minutes.

3 Combine equal parts by weight first of dried rose petals and gunpowder tea, and then of jasmine petals and the tea, adding a quarter part of dried lemon zest to the jasmine mixture. Store the teas in separate airtight containers.

HERB-INFUSED OILS

Now lighter, healthier dressings for salads are popular, these delicately flavoured oils make very welcome gifts. It is best to use only one variety of herb in each bottle of oil, but oregano and basil do go well together. Olive or sunflower oil is recommended, or use walnut or grapeseed for a gourmet treat.

YOU WILL NEED
Stems of fresh rosemary, thyme,
  oregano or basil
Paper towel
Attractive presentation bottles
Plastic or glass funnel
Scissors
Fine quality salad oils of your choice
Self-adhesive labels

1 Choose only the freshest stems of herbs, wash in cold water and pat dry on a paper towel.

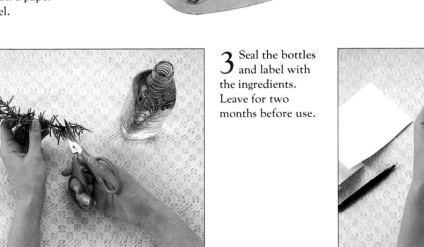

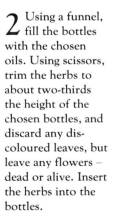

2 Using a funnel, fill the bottles with the chosen oils. Using scissors, trim the herbs to about two-thirds the height of the chosen bottles, and discard any discoloured leaves, but leave any flowers – dead or alive. Insert the herbs into the bottles.

3 Seal the bottles and label with the ingredients. Leave for two months before use.

CHOCOLATE FUDGE

This is a beautiful rich fudge, made in the traditional way. It will make a delectable gift for anyone with a sweet tooth.

YOU WILL NEED

450 g (1 lb/2¼ cups) granulated
    sugar (preferably cane)
150 ml (¼ pint/⅔ cup) milk
50 g (2 oz/¼ cup) cocoa powder
50 g (2 oz/2 squares) dark chocolate
Saucepan
6 drops vanilla essence (extract)
150 ml (¼ pint/⅔ cup) double (heavy)
    cream
100 g (4 oz/½ cup) unsalted butter
Shallow non-stick baking sheet
Metal spatula
Sharp knife
Gift boxes

2 The mixture will now be thick. Transfer to an oiled non-stick shallow baking sheet and spread out evenly using a metal spatula. Leave to set for 12 hours in a cool place.

1 Heat the sugar, milk, cocoa and chocolate in a pan, stirring until the mixture has dissolved. Add the vanilla essence, cream and the butter, then re-heat stirring occasionally until the butter melts. Remove from the heat and beat with a wooden spoon until the fudge mixture starts to granulate.

3 Invert the fudge onto a chopping board and cut into even squares, frequently dipping the knife blade in water. Pack into your chosen gift boxes.

TANGY VINEGARS

Flavoured red wine or cider vinegars are invaluable in preparing many dishes, sauces and dressings. They keep well for several months after maturing, but should be stored away from bright light. Here are recipes for tarragon vinegar and red chilli with ginger vinegar. Alternatives are numerous: try making a salad dressing with grapeseed oil and ginger and garlic vinegar, or tarragon vinegar and yogurt with cold chicken; or black pepper, coriander and cardamom vinegar in a meat stew; and red chilli and cumin vinegar on fried fish.

YOU WILL NEED
Fresh tarragon stems
Screw-topped bottle of cider vinegar
Whole dried red chillies
Fresh ginger root
Screw-topped bottle of red wine
  vinegar
Ribbon for decorating
Self-adhesive labels
Felt-tip pen

1 Trim three freshly picked tarragon stems to fit under the surface of the cider vinegar, and put into the bottle.

2 Place two whole red chillies and two small pieces of ginger root in a bottle of red wine vinegar.

3 Screw the lids onto the bottles, decorate with ribbon and add labels listing the ingredients. Store in a dark cool place for at least a month.

BOUQUET GARNI

The traditional bouquet garni is made from three sprigs of parsley, two of thyme and a bay leaf tied together with string, and often enclosed in muslin (cheesecloth) so that it can easily be removed. Other herbs may be added, such as fennel for fish dishes, three sage leaves for pork dishes, four short sprigs of rosemary for lamb dishes, two sprigs of fresh coriander (cilantro) and an extra bay leaf for beef dishes.

YOU WILL NEED
Sprigs of fresh or dried parsley and
   thyme
Bay leaf
Sharp pointed scissors
Muslin (cheesecloth)
White string

2 Cut out circles of muslin (cheesecloth) 9 cm (3½ in) in diameter.

Put two heaped teaspoons of the herbs into the centre of each circle.

1 Mix together three parts chopped parsley, two parts chopped thyme and one part broken bay leaves.

3 Gather the muslin around the herbs and tie in little bundles with white string. Store in an airtight container.

CHERRIES IN BRANDY

Only use the best quality canned cherries as cheaper varieties might split open in the brandy. A decorative jar filled with perfect fruit makes a most acceptable hostess gift.

YOU WILL NEED
1 can best quality pitted red cherries
  in syrup
Can opener
Small saucepan
1 cinnamon stick
3 tablespoons granulated cane sugar
Wooden spoon
Strainer
2 screw-top jars (sterilized)
¼ bottle of cooking brandy
3 drops vanilla essence (extract)
Small jug
Fancy lidded glass jar (sterilized)
Ribbon
Label

1 Drain the syrup from the cherries into a saucepan, add the cinnamon stick and sugar and stir continuously while bringing to the boil. Allow to cool and strain off into one of the screw-top jars and store in the refrigerator.

2 Reject any damaged fruit and place the remainder in the other screw-top jar. Add the brandy and vanilla essence. Screw on the lid and store in a cool place for 3-4 weeks.

3 Pour off the brandy into a jug, and stir in small quantities of the chilled syrup to taste. Place the cinnamon stick in the fancy glass jar and pack in the fruit in a decorative manner. Fill the container with the sweetened brandy, seal and finish with a ribbon bow. Add a label listing the ingredients.

FRILLY SOCKS

Transform a pair of white socks with frilled ribbon for a little girl to wear to a party.

YOU WILL NEED
2.5 m × 15 mm (2¾ yd × ⅝ in)
  narrow ribbon
Scissors
Needle and thread
Pins
Pair of plain socks

1 Cut the ribbon into six equal lengths. Sew a line of running stitches as near to one edge as possible of each piece of ribbon.

2 Pull the ribbon up the thread to gather the length of ribbon. Repeat with the other pieces of ribbon.

3 Starting at the back, pin the gathered edge of the ribbon to the top of the sock to hold it in place. When you have pinned the ribbon all the way round, make sure both ends overlap slightly.

4 Tack the ribbon in place and then secure it with a line of backstitch, stretching the sock as you work, so it will still fit over the child's ankle.

5 Sew on the other two lengths at 10 mm (⅜ in) intervals. Repeat with the other sock.

GIANT BOW

Make a giant bow to trim a gift-wrapped package. Choose colours that tone with the paper or make a good contrast.

YOU WILL NEED
2 m (2 yd) lengths of twisted paper
*   rope in 2 different colours*
2 m (2 yd) satin ribbon
Sticky tape

1 Untwist the lengths of coloured paper rope and spread them out.

2 Twist the paper rope strands together with the satin ribbon.

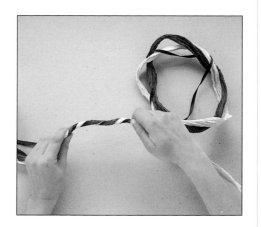

3 Wrap around the middle of a gift-wrapped package and tie the remaining loose untwisted ends into a bow. Use a small piece of sticky tape to fasten in place if necessary.

DRAUGHT
EXCLUDER

Make your home cosy and keep draughts at bay in a colourful way. Cushions in matching fabric would give a co-ordinated look.

YOU WILL NEED
Ruler
25 cm × 122 cm (¼ yd × 48 in) furnishing fabric
Scissors
Pins
Needle and thread
Wadding (batting) or stuffing
1.6 m (1¾ yd) wide ribbon

1 Measure the width of the door; upstairs doors are usually narrower than those downstairs. Allow an extra 18 cm (7 in) width for seam allowances and cut out the fabric to the required size. Turn in and pin 9 cm (3½ in) at each end and machine sew two rows of a long (gathering) stitch, stopping just short of the seam allowance. Pull the threads through to the right side of the fabric.

2 Fold in half lengthways, right sides together. Pin and machine along the edge, taking care not to stitch over the long threads.

3 Turn through to the right side and pull up the gathering threads at one end. Knot to fasten off.

4 Stuff from the open end until the 'sausage' feels firm. Pull up the gathering threads from the open end. Tie securely and fasten off.

5 Cut the ribbon in half and cut a 'V' shape in the ends. Tie an extravagant bow at each end of the 'sausage'.

LACE HANDKERCHIEF

It is very simple to add delicate detail to a plain handkerchief with a trimming of lace. Scraps of unusual or antique lace are worth collecting and saving for such a project.

YOU WILL NEED
21 cm (8½ in) square of Swiss lawn (fine cotton)
Steam iron
Tailor's chalk
Scissors
130 cm (51 in) fine cotton lace
Needle and thread

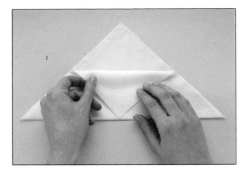

1 Fold the square of lawn into a triangle and press. Fold again to make a smaller triangle. Unfold once. Chalk the position of the lace inside one corner, chalking on both sides.

2 Cut off the corner of lawn along the chalked lines.

3 Pin a strip of lace along the raw edge allowing a 6 mm (¼ in) overlap on the lawn. Pin the lawn corner to the lace again allowing a 6 mm (¼ in) overlap. Secure with oversewing. Turn in the lawn overlap making a fine rolled hem along both sides, catching the edge of the lace at the same time.

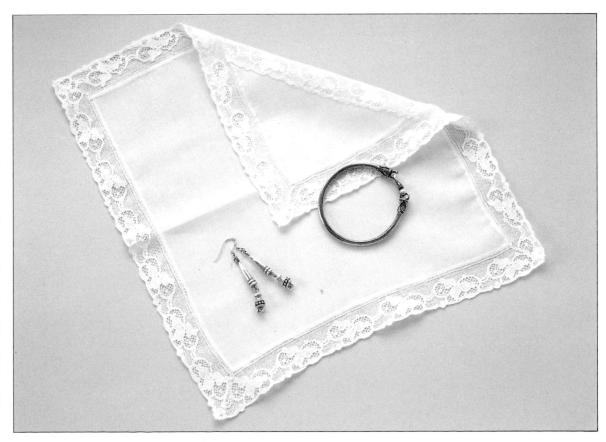

4 Sew four pieces of lace, each 28 cm (11 in) long, along each side of the handkerchief, leaving a 6 mm (¼ in) overlap. At each corner leave enough lace to overlap into a square. Trim the lace along the diagonal at each corner leaving 3 mm (⅛ in) overlapping. Hem the lawn overlap into a fine rolled edge along all four sides of the handkerchief. Neatly sew up the diagonal lace corners and sew the lace onto the hemmed edges.

STRAWBERRY BERET

1 Cut out some red strawberry shapes and green stems from the felt.

Berets are available in a wide range of colours and are not expensive. Appliquéd felt strawberries make an original decoration for this classic yet elegant hat.

YOU WILL NEED
Red and green felt
Scissors
Needle and thread
Miniature beads
Beret
Rubber-based glue

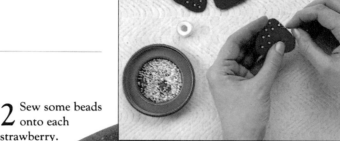

2 Sew some beads onto each strawberry.

3 Stick the motifs on the beret using rubber-based glue. Allow to dry.

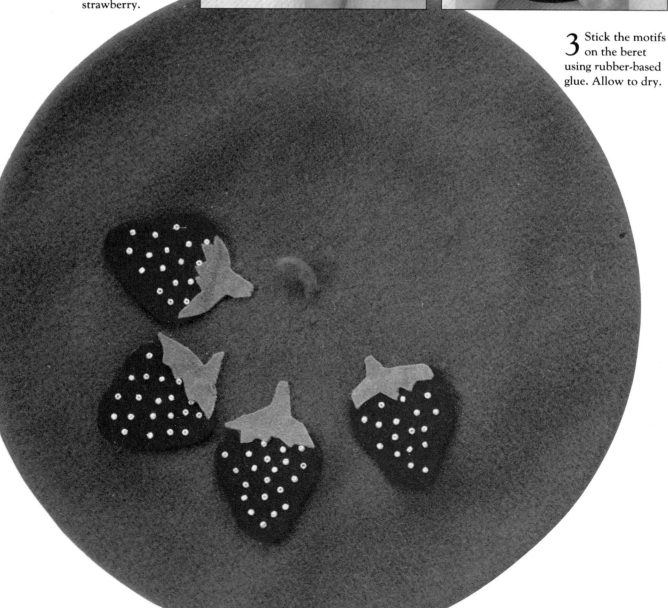

BERIBBONED
SPECTACLE CASE

Make this pretty padded case to protect a pair of glasses. Choose brightly coloured fabric and ribbons so that the case will always be easy to find!

YOU WILL NEED

4 pieces of fabric, each measuring 14 cm × 21 cm (5½ in × 8½ in)

2 pieces of foam interlining, each measuring 14 cm × 21 cm (5½ in × 8½ in)

Pins

Needle and thread

Metal rule

Scissors

1.6 m (64 in) length of wide ribbon

1.6 m (64 in) length of narrow ribbon

1 Place a rectangle of fabric on top of each piece of foam interlining so that they fit flush. Pin and tack (baste) in place.

2 Place the rectangles of fabric together. Pin and tack (baste). Sew around three sides with a 15 mm (⅝ in) seam allowance, leaving one short end open. Trim the seams. To make the ribbon front mark the front edge on the right side of one of the remaining rectangles of fabric 5 cm (2 in) from the top. Lay the first piece of ribbon from the corner to the mark. Secure with pins. Continue to lay the ribbon diagonally across the fabric, alternating the wide and narrow ribbons and leaving a gap of 5 mm (¼ in) between each ribbon. When you have reached the bottom of the material, do not forget to finish the top triangle. Tack (baste) into place.

3 Next, start weaving the ribbon in the opposite direction, again alternating between the narrow and wide ribbons. Secure with pins. When complete, tack (baste) into place and trim the ends.

4 Sew the ribbon side to the right side of the fabric rectangle. Sew around three sides, using a 20 mm (¾ in) allowance and leaving the bottom end open. Trim and turn through.

5 Use a closed pair of scissors to push the lining gently and carefully into place. Turn the raw ends under by 3 cm (1¼ in). Pin and stitch in place.

MAKE-UP BAG

This eye-catching make-up bag is made in quilted satin, with a contrasting zip and a co-ordinated lining.

YOU WILL NEED

25 cm × 115 cm (¼ yd × 45 in) satin
25 cm × 115 cm (¼ yd × 45 in) cotton lining
Flat wadding (batting) or flannelette
Scissors
Pins
Needle and thread
20 cm (8 in) zip
Tiny piece of ribbon

1 Cut out two pieces of satin and lining, each 20 cm × 15 cm (8 in × 6 in), and two pieces of wadding (batting) 20 cm × 14 cm (8 in × 5½ in). Pin and tack together the satin, wadding (batting) and lining, leaving a gap where the wadding (batting) does not reach to the top. This will make it easier to put in the zip.

2 Quilt by hand or machine. Fold in the top edges of the bag and tack in place.

3 Lay the zip right side up and place the two folded sides of the bag over it. Pin, tack and sew in place. If you use a machine, attach the zipper foot. Open the zip, then turn the bag through right sides together. Pin, tack and sew around the sides and base edge. Trim then overstitch to neaten. Trim the corners diagonally and turn through to the right side. Tie a tiny piece of ribbon to the zip pull for decoration.

PADDED COAT HANGER

Padded coat hangers are a must for the well-dressed person, preventing clothes from having hanging marks on the shoulders. These are both decorative and easy to sew. You could also add some pot-pourri in the hanger for a scented gift.

YOU WILL NEED

140 cm × 10 cm (55 in × 4 in) wadding (batting) or a double thickness strip the same size as the coat hanger
Wooden coat hanger
Needle and thread
Iron
60 cm × 15 cm (24 in × 6 in) strip of fabric
Pins
Ribbon

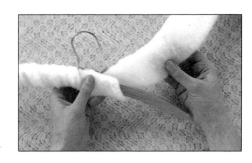

1 Wind the length of wadding (batting) around the coat hanger, making sure it is even. Sew the ends in place.

2 Press in a seam allowance of about 6 mm (¼ in) on all four sides of the strip of fabric.

3 Mark the centre with a pin. Fold the fabric around the hanger with the open edge at the top. Using a double thread, start at one end and sew a running stitch from one end up to the centre. Repeat, starting at the other end.

4 Gather up each end so that it curves around the hanger. Sew to fasten securely. Wrap the hook in green ribbon and sew in the end.

PEG BAG

Hanging out your washing on the line is easier if the clothes pegs are kept in a special bag. A rotary cutter and self-heal mat help to ensure the quick and accurate cutting of fabric for patchwork.

YOU WILL NEED

Saw
Wooden coat hanger
Tape measure
Rotary cutter or scissors
30 cm × 115 cm (⅓ yd × 45 in) patterned fabric
25 cm × 115 cm (¼ yd × 45 in) contrasting plain fabric
50 cm × 115 cm (½ yd × 45 in) lining
Needle and thread
Steam iron
Pair of compasses
Pencil
Ruler
Tracing paper
Pins
Bias binding

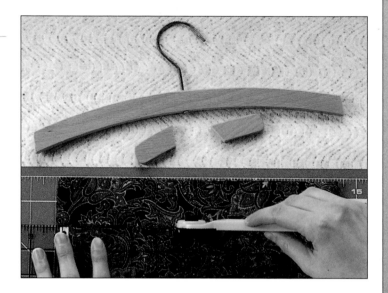

1 Using a saw, cut off the ends of the coat hanger so that it measures 33 cm (13 in). Cut out five strips measuring 70 cm × 5 cm (28 in × 2 in) of the patterned fabric and four identical strips of the plain fabric. Cut out a 70 cm × 35 cm (28 in × 13½ in) piece of lining.

2 Sew the strips in pairs with a 6 mm (¼ in) seam allowance until all nine are joined. Press the seams open. Trim the ends straight.

3 Draw a 15 cm (6 in) diameter circle on tracing paper and cut out. Place the lining right side down and the joined strips right side up on top. Place the template 7.5 cm (3 in) from the top and equidistant from the sides. Pin the two layers of fabric around the circle to stop them from moving, then draw around the template in pencil. Cut out the circle.

4 Measure the circumference of the circle and cut a piece of bias binding slightly larger. Join with a diagonal seam.

5 Pin, tack and sew the bias binding in place.

6 Fold the fabric in half right sides together, keeping the circular opening at the top. Place the coat hanger at the top and mark the curve of the hanger using a pencil. Cut just outside this line leaving about 6 mm (¼ in) seam allowance. Pin the three sides and sew, leaving a gap for the hook at the top. Trim the corners diagonally. Zigzag stitch around to neaten the seams. Turn through and insert the coat hanger.

PATCHWORK CUSHION

This striking design is surprisingly quick to make, using just one template. Experiment with placing the strips of triangles in different combinations.

YOU WILL NEED
Template plastic
Pencil
Ruler
Pieces of black and white fabrics, each about 36 cm × 18 cm (14 in × 7 in)
White pencil
Scissors
Pins
Patchwork square rule
25 cm × 115 cm (¼ yd × 45 in) turquoise fabric
25 cm × 115 cm (¼ yd × 45 in) blue fabric
Needle and thread
Iron
164 cm (64 in) strip of striped fabric
38 cm (15 in) cushion pad

1 Using the template as a guide and including 6 mm (¼ in) seam allowance, draw 20 triangles on the black fabric and 20 on the white, having first drawn two parallel lines along the grain of each fabric in which to fit the triangles.

2 Cut out and pin the triangles in pairs of one black and one white, keeping the straight grain along the top and bottom. Continue to pin pairs until you have four strips of five pairs. Each alternate strip should start with a white triangle and finish with a black one.

3 Pin the strips together, offsetting the black points to the centre of the black triangle in the next row.

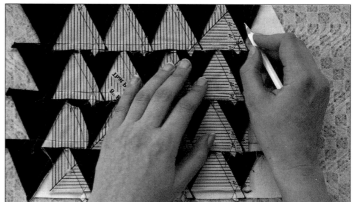

4 Using a patchwork square rule draw a 20 cm (8 in) square plus 6 mm (¼ in) seam allowance on the wrong side, centred so that the points of the triangles balance. These lines will be your stitching lines. Trim to 6 mm (¼ in) seam allowance.

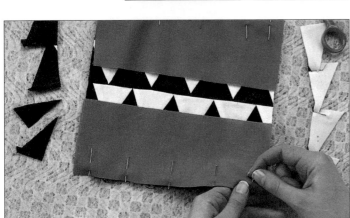

5 Measure opposite sides of the square and cut two strips of turquoise fabric 9 cm (3½ in) wide to fit. Pin with right sides together, sew and press flat. Measure remaining sides and cut two strips of blue fabric 9 cm (3½ in) wide to fit. Pin with right sides together, sew and press flat.

6 Continue in the same manner, cutting black and white striped fabric 3 cm (1¼ in) wide to fit. Pin, sew and press. To make the back of the cover, cut a piece of blue fabric to fit the width plus 6 mm (¼ in) seam allowance. Cut a piece of turquoise fabric of the same width but longer for the overlap. Turn in a hem at one end of each piece. Place the two pieces, right sides together, over the patchwork square. Pin, sew and snip off the corners diagonally, so that the corners will be sharp. Invert and press. Insert the cushion pad.

FELT NEEDLECASE

Make this attractive needlecase from brightly coloured scraps of felt to keep your sewing and embroidery needles safe.

YOU WILL NEED
Stiff white card
Ruler
Scissors
Small pieces of fuchsia, pink, orange, green and yellow felt
Black felt-tip pen
Coin
Stranded cotton in yellow, orange and green
Crewel needle
Tacking (basting) thread in a contrasting colour
Sewing needle

1 Cut out a 9 cm × 14 cm (3½ in × 5½ in) rectangle from white card to make a template. Lay the template on the fuchsia felt, draw round it with the black felt-tip pen and cut out. Repeat with the pink and orange felt.

2 Using a coin as a template, cut out a circle of both the green and yellow felt. Also cut out a small strip and a square of the fuchsia felt.

Arrange the shapes on half of the pink felt rectangle and attach them using blanket stitch and three strands of cotton with the crewel needle.

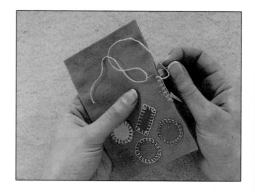

3 Tack (baste) the pink and fuchsia felt rectangles together. Work a row of blanket stitch round the edge using three strands of yellow thread. With the fuchsia side facing, stitch the orange felt down the centre, then fold in half to make a book shape. You may need to trim the orange felt slightly round the edges with sharp scissors.

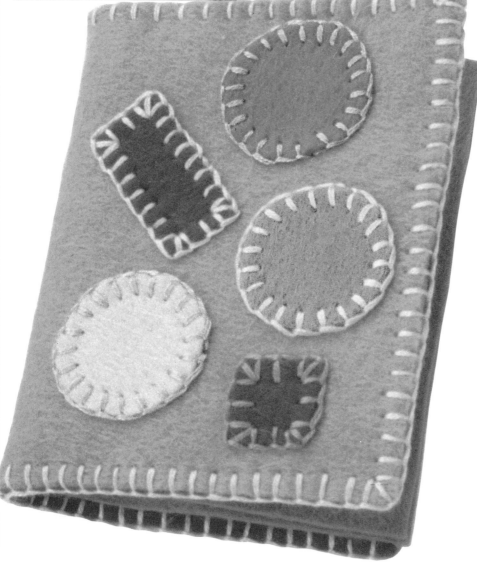

HEART-SHAPED BOX

A porcelain box with an embroidered design set in the lid makes a lovely gift for a special friend. Fill the box with pot-pourri or some favourite bath pearls.

YOU WILL NEED

Tracing paper
Sharp HB pencil
Small piece of pink cotton or linen
*   fabric*
Stranded cotton in yellow, pink, light
*   green and jade green*
Crewel needle
Tapestry needle
Steam iron
Scissors
Heart-shaped porcelain craft box in
*   pink*

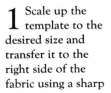

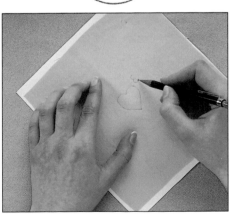

1 Scale up the template to the desired size and transfer it to the right side of the fabric using a sharp HB pencil. Make sure you transfer each part of the design, including the heart-shaped cutting line.

2 Following the colours shown on the template, embroider the design in whipped backstitch, chain stitch and French knots, using two strands of thread in the crewel needle. When working the whipping stage of the backstitch, use six strands of thread in the tapestry needle.

3 Press the embroidery lightly on the wrong side with a cool iron. Cut out along the heart-shaped cutting line with a pair of sharp scissors. Mount the embroidery in the box lid following the manufacturer's instructions.

SILVER PENDANT

A silver-plated pendant is the perfect way to display a tiny piece of beautifully stitched embroidery with a small-scale design.

YOU WILL NEED

Oval silver-plated craft pendant and chain
Small piece of 18-count ainring in white
Sharp HB pencil
Stranded cotton in yellow, orange, light green and dark green
Crewel needle
Scissors

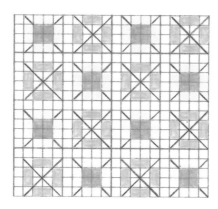

1 Remove the card shape from the pendant and lay it on the fabric. Draw round the card with a pencil.

2 Each coloured square on the chart represents one cross stitch worked over one woven block in the fabric. Following the chart, embroider the design in cross stitch using two strands of thread. Embroider the linear details in half cross stitch worked over one fabric block using two strands of dark green thread.

3 Cut out the embroidery slightly inside the pencil line. Mount in the pendant following the manufacturer's instructions.

CHRISTMAS TREE DECORATIONS

Hand-embroidered Christmas decorations in shaped golden frames will make your tree trimming a talking point year after year.

YOU WILL NEED

Small pieces of 11-count pearl aida in white

Stranded cotton in red, dark red, light green, mid green, dark green and brown

Tapestry needle

Metallic-effect gold yarn

Small gold beads

Shaped gold-coloured craft Christmas frames with shaped red felt self-adhesive backing

Sharp HB pencil

Scissors

Narrow red ribbon for hanging

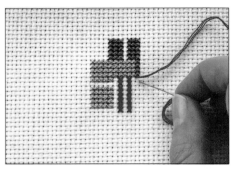

1 Each coloured square on the chart represents one cross stitch worked over one woven block in the fabric. Work the designs in cross stitch using three strands of thread (or one strand of gold yarn).

2 Outline the striped package in backstitch using two strands of brown thread. Add straight stitches and beads to the tree design.

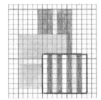

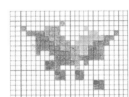

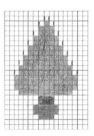

3 Centre the frames over the embroidered motifs and draw round the outsides with a sharp HB pencil.

4 Cut out the embroideries slightly inside the pencil lines. Mount in the frames following the manufacturer's instructions. To finish, add the red felt backing and red ribbon for hanging.

TRINKET ROLL

A pretty and practical way to store your treasures when on holiday, this roll has two fat 'sausages' for rings and earrings, and a pocket for necklaces and bracelets.

YOU WILL NEED

Scissors
Ruler
30 cm × 115 cm (⅓ yd × 45 in) velvet
30 cm × 115 cm (⅓ yd × 45 in) lining
Pins
Iron
Needle and thread
18 cm (7 in) zip
2.5 m × 15 mm (2¾ yd × ⅝ in) bias binding
Small piece of velcro

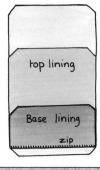

1 Cut out one piece of velvet 33 cm × 23 cm (13 in × 9 in) and round off the four corners. Cut out two pieces of lining 25 cm × 23 cm (10 in × 9 in), and three pieces 23 cm × 11.5 cm (9 in × 4½ in) of velvet. One of these is a pocket and the others are tubes for rings and earrings.

2 Press in two edges of the lining, centre and place the zip between. Pin and sew in place. Curve the corners to fit the velvet top.

3 Cut a length of bias binding to fit the velvet pocket and press in half. Fold over the pocket, pin and sew on. Place the pocket on the lining, wrong side up and sew along the bottom. Bring the pocket up and pin the end before tacking (basting) in place.

4 Roll the last two velvet pieces into sausage shapes, pin and slip stitch.

5 Sew velcro to the end of the one for rings and sew the corresponding piece onto the lining.

6 Pin the lining onto the wrong side of the velvet, making sure the two sausage shapes are in place. Measure enough bias binding to fit around the edge and leave a length for the ties. Fold the ties in half lengthways and sew. Pin the ties to the centre of one end of the roll. Place the binding, right sides together, on the velvet and pin, then tack (baste) and sew in place. Fold over to the inside and slip stitch. Check that you have caught the edges of the pocket and the 'sausage' for earrings on both sides, but on only one side for the 'sausage' for rings.

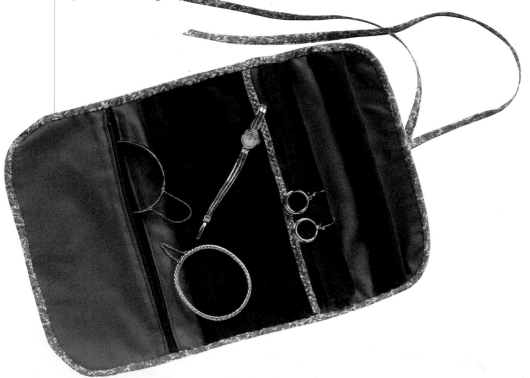

QUILTED CUSHION COVER

Scraps of furnishing fabric are excellent for making this comfortable quilted cushion cover. The quilting helps it to keep its shape well. The measurements can easily be altered to fit any size of cushion pad; try making an assortment to pile on a comfortable sofa.

YOU WILL NEED

Furnishing fabric in two patterns
Metal rule
Scissors
Needle and thread
Steam iron
45 cm (18 in) square of foam interlining
45 cm (18 in) square of backing fabric
1 m (1 yd) ribbon
41 cm (16 in) cushion pad

1 Cut out four squares measuring 15 cm (6 in) and one measuring 23 cm (9 in) of one pattern of furnishing fabric, making sure that the pattern is following the same direction. Cut out two pieces measuring 15 cm (6 in) long and 23 cm (9 in) wide and two pieces measuring 23 cm (9 in) long and 15 cm (6 in) wide of the other pattern of furnishing fabric, again making sure that the pattern is following the same direction. Sew the pieces of fabric together using a 20 mm (¾ in) seam allowance. Press open the seams. Sew the panels together using the same seam allowance and press open.

2 Lay the cushion front on the interlining, pin together and tack (baste). Machine sew very carefully along each seam line to create a padded appearance.

4 Make small bows from the ribbon and stitch into place. Push the cushion pad through the opening, making sure the pad is pushed into the corners. Once in position, slipstitch the opening.

3 With right sides together, pin and tack (baste) the backing fabric to the front. Sew together using a 20 mm (¾ in) seam allowance but leave an opening of about 20 cm (8 in) to enable the cover to be turned through. Trim the corners and seams. Turn through.

INDEX